Portsmouth
CITY COUNCIL
Leisure Service

People of Portsmouth

The 20th Century in Their Own Words

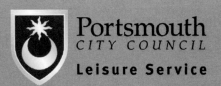

Portsmouth
CITY COUNCIL
Leisure Service

People of Portsmouth

*The 20th Century in
Their Own Words*

Edited by John Stedman
PORTSMOUTH MUSEUMS AND RECORDS SERVICE

breedon **books**
PUBLISHING

First published in Great Britain in 2002 by
The Breedon Books Publishing Company Limited
Breedon House, 3 The Parker Centre,
Derby, DE21 4SZ.

Dedication
For everyone who shared their
memories with us,
and for all the people of
Portsmouth.

ISBN 1 85983 317 9

Printed and bound by Butler & Tanner, Frome,
Somerset, England.

Cover printing by Lawrence-Allen Colour Printers,
Weston-super-Mare, Somerset, England.

CONTENTS

Editor's Note

THIS book is a history of Portsmouth based on the memories of inhabitants of the city. A great number of local people have generously shared their recollections with us, and allowed them to be recorded on tape or minidisc. Most of the words that follow are quoted from these recordings.

Recording interviews about people's lives is a technique of historical research known as 'oral history'. It has become widely adopted only since the 1970s, but spoken memories are the oldest form of history. Only the tape recorder is new. The passing of knowledge from one person to another by the spoken word is

the oldest of traditions, predating the invention of handwriting. It remains the basis of our system of justice, through the retelling of what they remember by witnesses in court. Memory is, of course, sometimes fallible and some things are more clearly remembered than others – experiences better than dates, for example. Yet, recorded memories allow us to understand more fully what it was like to live in the past than the documents that conventional historians use.

Some of the interviews were recorded specially for the book, others were made for earlier projects. All but a few are from the collections of either Ports-

mouth City Council's museums and records service, a division of its Leisure Service, or the Portsmouth Royal Dockyard Historical Trust, which exists to preserve the history of the dockyard. These two collections now include over 900 interviews. The recordings and transcripts, and also many of the photographs reproduced in the book, can be consulted in the searchroom of the City Museum & Records Office, Museum Road, Old Portsmouth. It is open Monday to Friday, 10am to 4pm. Other interviews with Portsmouth people can be heard at the Wessex Film & Sound Archive, Hampshire County Record Office, Winchester.

Acknowledgements

WE WOULD like to thank all the many people whose contributions and help have made it possible for us to compile this book. Foremost, we owe a great debt to everyone who has allowed us and our colleagues to record their memories over the last couple of decades, both for this book and for other projects. We hope they enjoyed the experience as much as we did. A considerable number of people have helped indirectly by transcribing or cataloguing recordings, which has made them much more accessible. The Portsmouth Royal Dockyard

Historical Trust have kindly given permission for us to use interviews from its extensive archive.

Thanks are also due to everyone who allowed us to copy photos and documents for the

book. Most of the images are from Portsmouth Museums & Records Service's collections, but *The News*, Portsmouth, has once more generously allowed us to reproduce pictures that are its copyright.

The Hard and dockyard main gate, 1905.

INTRODUCTION
A CENTURY OF CHANGE

NO COMMUNITY CAN PASS THROUGH A PERIOD AS LONG AS A CENTURY WITHOUT EXPERIENCING CHANGE TO SOME DEGREE, BUT IN PORTSMOUTH'S CASE THIS CHANGE WAS DRAMATICALLY RAPID AND FAR-REACHING. THE CENTURY WAS A WATERSHED IN THE CITY'S HISTORY. THIS BOOK CHRONICLES SOME OF THOSE CHANGES AND EXPLORES THE IMPACT THEY HAD ON PORTSMOUTH PEOPLE'S LIVES, LARGELY USING THEIR OWN WORDS.

FROM the 17th century until 1939 the population of Portsmouth grew dramatically and seemingly inexorably. The stimulus was war, and the preparation for war: when Britain went to war the dockyard needed extra labour. By 1900 the town's population had reached 186,000, the 1931 census put it at 249,283 and it was estimated to be about 260,000 in 1939. This increase was largely due to migration from other parts of the United Kingdom, including from dockyards in Ireland and Wales that closed in the 1920s. There were so many Welsh, Scots, Devonians, Cornishmen and Lancastrians that each group of exiles had their own social club for sports and dances.

The war years, however, saw a decrease in Portsmouth's population and in the following decades the decline continued. This fall was due to several

HMS *Nelson* entering Portsmouth Harbour about 1937. Most of the houses in the foreground were destroyed in World War Two.

factors. The war was one of them. German bombing wrought terrible destruction in the city. The council recorded 930 civilians killed. Although the casualties among Portsmouth men and women in the armed forces were nowhere near as high as during World War One, still many died, creating hundreds of widows and orphans. One in ten of the city's houses were destroyed and as many again seriously damaged. Many families moved out to the surrounding districts, some just while the bombing lasted, others permanently. Yet more were relocated to other naval bases.

More important in the long run, however, was the council's decision to relieve crowding on Portsea Island by clearing areas of dense housing and rebuilding more spaciously. Areas of densely packed terraced housing, mostly old and well below modern standards, were designated 'slums' and demolished. New housing was provided at sites off Portsea Island, at Paulsgrove and outside the city boundary, at Leigh Park and Wecock Farm. Many of Portsmouth's more prosperous inhabitants moved to privately developed districts at Portchester, Waterlooville or Horndean. As more people could afford cars, the size of the Portsmouth's travel-to-work-area increased. Before 1939 the city had preserved its population as its built-up area spread by extending the city boundaries: in 1904 to embrace all Portsea Island, in 1920 taking in Cosham and Paulsgrove, and in 1932 Drayton and eastern Portchester.

Inter-war suburban development on the mainland, with Drayton Methodist Church (centre).

Resistance from other local authorities prevented similar expansion after 1945.

Not until 1991 did the census again record an upturn in the number of the city's inhabitants. Growth has continued since then, again at least partly due to migration. Some of the new incomers are students, recruited from all across the world as the university has sought to raise income. More permanent newcomers have been immigrants from overseas who have come both to take advantage of the better opportunities offered and, in some cases, to escape oppressive regimes. They hail mostly from former parts of the

British Empire, such as Zanzibar, but in recent years there have been many refugees from conflicts in Europe. In 2000 some 37 different languages were spoken by Portsmouth citizens. The biggest groups of incomers are of Bangladeshi, Chinese or Vietnamese origins.

The status of the town saw several changes. In 1900 Portsmouth was a County Borough, effectively independent of Hampshire County Council. This arrangement continued until 1974, when Portsmouth lost control of schools, libraries, social services and some planning responsibilities to the county council. All these were recovered in 1997 when Portsmouth became one of the new unitary local authorities. The town became a city in 1926, and the mayor was awarded the title of Lord Mayor in 1928.

In political life, the Conservative Party dominated Portsmouth for most of the 20th century. They not only provided most of the city's MPs, they also controlled the council until 1994, except in 1964–65. The identification of the Conservatives as the party of high defence expenditure undoubtedly gave them great appeal in a community dominated by dockyard workers and servicemen. The story of the town's Liberals followed the fortunes of the national party. Sir Thomas Bramsdon, who lost his seat in the election of 1924, was the last Liberal MP for 73 years. His successor, Mike Hancock, began as a Labour councillor, but joined the Social Democratic Party on its formation and won Portsmouth South in 1984. He retook the seat as a Liberal Democrat in 1997. By 1945 Labour had become the natural party of opposition on the council, but the Liberals staged a comeback in the 1990s, obtaining power again in alliance with Labour. The first Labour MP, W.J. Hall, was elected in 1929, and the party took two of the city's three seats in the Labour landslide of 1945. Between 1950 and 1997 the party had only one local MP, Frank Judd, who held office between 1966 and 1979.

Paradoxically, although governed by Conservative politicians, Portsmouth has long experienced 'municipal socialism', in which significant parts of the town's infrastructure were run by the council, not by private enterprise. Sewage disposal remained a local government operation until its compulsory privatisation in the 1980s by Margaret Thatcher's government. The council decided to erect a power station itself in 1894 rather than allow a private company to do the job. The City of Portsmouth Electricity Department provided power for a growing area of south-east Hampshire until the creation of the Central Electricity Generating Board in 1948. The power station was demolished in 1977. In 1901 the council took over, by compulsory purchase, the tramway system and electrified it, running the trams, the trolleybuses and motor buses that succeeded them, again until privatisation in the 1980s. Commercial quays at the Camber and Flathouse were already under its control, but in 1968 the council built a new quay at Rudmore and, in 1976, constructed an international ferry terminal. Before the formation of the NHS, St James' Hospital was also a council responsibility. Finally, the corporation even ran part of the local telephone system, establishing a local exchange in 1900 that was taken over by the GPO in 1913.

The dockyard dominated the city's economy until the late 20th century. In periods of expansion, such as the race with Germany to build dreadnoughts before World War One, and the rearmament of the late 1930s, Portsmouth flourished. When employment and expenditure in the dockyard fell, as it did in the 1920s, there was poverty in the town. The yard employed thousands of men, almost 8,000 in 1901 and 15,000 in 1914, falling after 1919, but reaching at least 22,000 by 1945. Their work was a mixture of building new vessels for the Royal Navy and maintaining the existing fleet. But the last vessel to be constructed in Portsmouth, the frigate *Andromeda*, came off the slip in 1967, and, in 1982, the dockyard was officially downgraded to a naval base. The number of employees now stands at less than 2,000. Admiralty policy was to keep the yard very largely self-contained, buying little from local suppliers, so there was not much economic spin-off to benefit the town's businesses. Wages were comparatively low albeit steady.

The dockyard affected the town's economy indirectly in a number of ways. Perhaps the most important was in women's work. Employment in the dockyard and navy was predominantly male. As a result women's wages in Portsmouth were comparatively low and that attracted corset manufacturers to the town. The trade was very extensive until the 1960s and persists in the city to this day.

Second, the council was well aware that the town's economy had to diversify if Portsmouth was to avoid being too reliant on the dockyard. The council began promoting Southsea as a seaside resort even before it became legal for the council to spend money doing it. When, in 1904, South

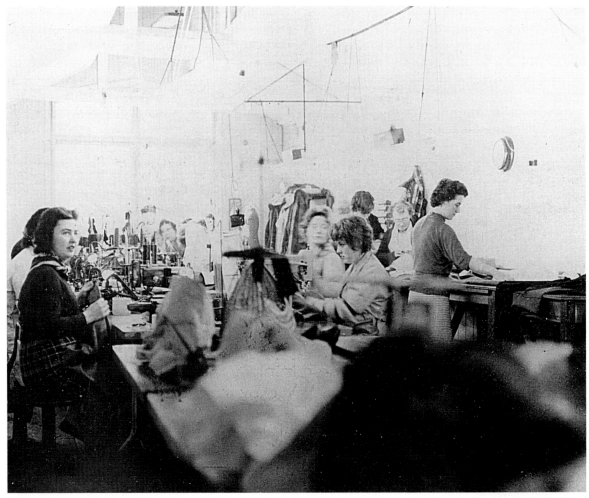

The workroom at Shimbart's, a naval tailors, in the 1980s.

Parade Pier was seriously damaged in a fire, the council bought and rebuilt the structure. In 1910 mixed bathing was permitted. Southsea Common was bought from the government in 1922 and improved with gardens, sports facilities and a bandstand. Soon there was a miniature railway (and another near Hilsea Lido) and a children's paddling pool. Music and variety shows at the theatre on South Parade Pier were extremely popular from the 1920s to the 1960s. After World War Two new developments included a roller-skating rink around the bandstand, marionette shows at the Rock Gardens Pavilion (which incorporated a restaurant), beauty pageants and the rebuilding of Clarence Pier, which had been bombed. By the late 1960s such attractions could not counteract the lure of package holidays abroad in the sun. From the 1970s the city's maritime heritage has been seen as one means of attracting visitors, thus the decline of the dockyard was partially compensated for by the release for public use of its oldest buildings. A trust was established to look after these important historic structures and the *Mary Rose* and HMS *Warrior* found homes there. There are now 14 museums, 'heritage attractions' and public art galleries within the city boundaries, and six others in Gosport, Fareham and Havant.

There were other attempts to diversify the city economy. They included the creation of an airport on farmland in the north-east of Portsea Island in 1932. It attracted new companies, such as Airspeed, later absorbed by de Havilland, which employed several thousand people on the

An Airspeed Courier capable of carrying five passengers, operated from Portsmouth airport by Portsmouth & Isle of Wight Aviation, about 1938.

book than there were in the 1901 Kelly's directory. The century began with a spate of work: the completion of the Roman Catholic cathedral, new Anglican churches such as St Patrick's and St Margaret's, Eastney, St Alban's and St Cuthbert's in Copnor, and St John's, Rudmore, Trinity Methodist Church, Albert Road, and the Roman Catholic church of St Joseph, Copnor. Most of these new buildings were in districts only recently developed and met the needs of the town's expanding population. In the inter-war period there were fewer new churches, even where new houses were going up; St Philip's Church (Anglican) on the Highbury estate, and St Colman's (Roman Catholic), both Cosham, and Drayton Methodist Church are some of only a handful of exceptions. St Thomas' church, in Old Portsmouth, was raised to a cathedral, however, in 1927, being picked over St Mary's,

site, Fireproof Tanks, an offshoot of Airspeed, and Hants & Sussex Aviation, still reconditioning aircraft engines. Portsmouth airport lasted only 41 years. The success of Channel Airways, operating from there in the 1960s, encouraged it to buy bigger planes, but the airfield's grass runways proved inadequate for them in wet weather and two crashed. The company relocated to Eastleigh and Portsmouth airport never recovered. Most of the site became an industrial estate, another arm in the council's attempts to encourage alternative employment. The first industrial estate, at Fratton, was started in 1947: there are now over 20. Two of the most successful areas in which new employers have been brought to Portsmouth are in defence work, of which the most notable was Marconi, and computing, as Portsmouth is home to IBM's UK headquarters.

Our perception of the 20th century as an age when spiritual life became less significant to most people is arguably supported by the history of church building in the city. There are certainly many fewer places of worship listed in the telephone

St Alban's Church, Copnor, after wartime damage was repaired.

Work proceeding on the platform for Portsmouth's millennium tower, early summer 2002.

Kingston, so the important parish work of the latter would not be disturbed. An extension of its nave was begun, but not finished, at the outbreak of World War Two. The war led to destruction of churches in southern Portsmouth, St John's, Portsea, and Elm Grove Baptist church, for example. Many were not rebuilt as their congregations had shrunk or moved. Instead new churches were built to serve the new estates at Leigh Park and Paulsgrove. The diocese of Portsmouth was unable to finish St Thomas's cathedral until 1990-1, probably because the designs proposed in the 1960s were so controversial. The new immigrant communities have brought their own faiths with them. The Muslim community has flourished to the extent that it is replacing a mosque in a pair of converted houses in Marmion Road with a new, larger mosque in a former cinema.

The city has had also a place on the national stage. The Solent has been the preferred venue for all the major naval reviews of the 20th century: Edward VII's review of 1908, the jubilee review of 1935, Queen Elizabeth's coronation review, the NATO review of 1969 and Silver Jubilee review of 1977. It was off Portsmouth that several of the Schneider Trophy seaplane races were held, culminating in the famous final victory by the Supermarine seaplane in 1931 that gave Britain permanent possession of the trophy. In 1994 the city hosted the international commemorations marking the 50th anniversary of D-Day, and one of the British legs of the Tour de France. More humbly, but perhaps having greater effect on people's daily lives, self-service shopping was pioneered in a PIMCO store in Albert Road, in 1947.

In spite of all this change, throughout the century, Portsmouth has retained much of its personality. It is still predominantly a city of small terraced houses, its population the most densely packed in England outside London. Its city centre is on a human scale. It has retained its close ties with the navy and, although there are no longer great numbers of sailors and dockyardmen among its citizens, that link has been reinforced by understanding of the importance of that naval heritage.

FAMILY AND COMMUNITY

**Sue Bruley,
Ligia Kašanin
and Gail
Stewart-Bye**

THE city is made up of many different communities meshed together by ties of kinship, school, work, religion and neighbourliness. Over the century it has spilled over into outlying areas, building up new communities in Waterlooville, Cosham, Leigh Park, Farlington and Paulsgrove. Although many of their inhabitants commute into Portsmouth for work, the centre has continued to attract residents, thus preserving its identity as a dynamic, living city. Over the century the character of family and community life has changed a great deal within this urban centre. The sprawling family of the late-Victorian era living a hand-to-mouth existence has been replaced by the modern, small nuclear family, often with both parents working. The domestic labour required in family life has been dramatically

Three generations of the Young family, about 1928.

reduced. Although women's lives are no longer circumscribed by never-ending domestic toil, they still tend to be responsible for keeping the wheels of the home turning. Street life has become less vigorous as families often choose to 'keep themselves to themselves'. More comfortable accommodation, the rise of the motor car and the advent of television and other home entertainment has led to fewer

children playing in the streets. In addition, higher living standards have meant that families and neighbours are no longer woven together by complex sets of interlocking duties and responsibilities which were the essential fabric of survival in working-class communities. Increased geographic and occupational mobility has aided these developments; Mum, Gran or Auntie no longer live a few doors or streets away. Nowadays people do not always know who their neighbours are. The Church has also been affected by these changes and is generally not nearly so significant in people's lives now as it was in 1900. Patterns of consumption have changed beyond recognition; from reliance on the corner shop to the supermarket in the 1960s and more recently to huge 'out-of-town' retail parks. With the decline of the dockyard and the growth of the college to university status, many households now consist of students rather than families. There have also been many migrants to Portsmouth making it a much more cosmopolitan city in the latter half of the century than previously.

Family life

Mum was the central pivot around which the family revolved. Above all, she had to make ends meet and get the family through the week on very limited resources. In the case of navy families mum often had to manage for long periods on her own. Her primary responsibility was to manage the household and this often meant that she had little time for shows of affection or for engaging in play.

We were very lucky really. In fact, I don't think I had a really deprived childhood. It may have been hard. Money was scarce, but it was not deprived at all. There

Joy Hobbs in her Girl Guide uniform, 1930s.

was enough. I suppose my mother was a good manager. She used to make everything, like they did in those days, all the sewing and that. (*Anonymous, born 1917 in Portsea*)

I loved being with my father. He was very good, very patient. Because I liked being with him,

liked doing things with him, he taught me to use tools and I had my own set, a little plane, a little chisel and screwdriver and a small hammer. He would give me a piece of wood and tell me to get on with it. I learnt a lot, because, although it wasn't his trade, he was a good woodworker. He used to do all

Mrs Voss wearing the kimono her husband brought home for her after a long spell serving on a warship in the Far East, 1936.

Dad used to work from early, five in the morning until about nine at night, ever since we were little. He was hardly there, we used to see him for about, I don't know, half an hour. Kirsty, my little sister used to see him hardly ever. (*Arran Stevens, child in the 1980s*)

Because Dad was away at sea Mum had to try and keep control. And as we got older we used to get slapped on the legs and stuff like that, if she was really cross with us, sent to our room, possibly, during the day. But the trouble was that she found that sending me to my room was ineffective because I'd just lie there and read. (*Neville Penter, child in the 1960s*)

I do remember going to Gran's, and I remember Mum used to go round there. And, as Gran got older, she used to do her work. Gran used to make this roast, and I used to go to the butcher's shop to get half a leg of lamb. I think it was 1s 6d. And Gran used to roast this with the potatoes and all that sort of thing. And then she used to make a bread pudding, and there was us three there. Mum had done all her work and that. Oh we did used to enjoy that! We used to think it was lovely, you know, that one day in the week when we used to go round to Gran's. (*Anonymous, born Portsea, 1917*)

the painting and decorating in the house. He taught himself to grain and varnish. So I learnt to paint and paper-hang. My first remembrance of helping was sitting on the stairs with a roll of paper and a pair of scissors. You didn't buy trimmed paper in those days... so I would sit and trim the paper and have to be very careful about it. (*Joy Hobbs, child in the 1920s–'30s*)

We had five families in Wilson Road. There was our house and then three of the brothers lived there and my grandmother with one of the daughters. We used to walk in and out of each other's houses. We had a system of straps on the door which you could pull and the latch came up. (*Doris Bealing, child in Stamshaw in the 1930s*)

The home, meals and cooking

At the turn of the century mothers laboured long hours preparing meals from fresh, raw ingredients. Gradually labour-saving devices and the advent of frozen food and prepared meals has meant that cooking time has been greatly reduced. Portsmouth families nowadays eat a much greater variety of food than they used to, including many meals of foreign origin such as curries, pasta and pizza. Family meals have also become more relaxed occasions, although perhaps some of the intimacy of family life has been lost as a result. In the early 20th century the kitchen range was often in what we would now call the living room.

You always had in that a scrubbed kitchen table and everything went on it. When you set the table you had a posh white cloth, and then, when that came off, you had one with chenille baubles all around it. Everybody had the same. Everything was done on that table. In the evening, you had no television or anything like that, so consequently, you all played cards or ludo or whatever it was – dominoes or something like that. (*Anonymous, born 1917*)

You just had the coal fire, the open fire in the front room. Nothing in the kitchen, no heating except for the stove. In the winter I would put that on first thing in the morning. But really you took the cold in your stride in those days... (*Jean Martin-Bennan, moved to Leigh Park in the 1950s*)

We had an old sofa. My grandmother used to love her sofa. She always used to have a sleep on the sofa in the afternoon. I used to like laying on there and listening to the radio as well. She also had a little

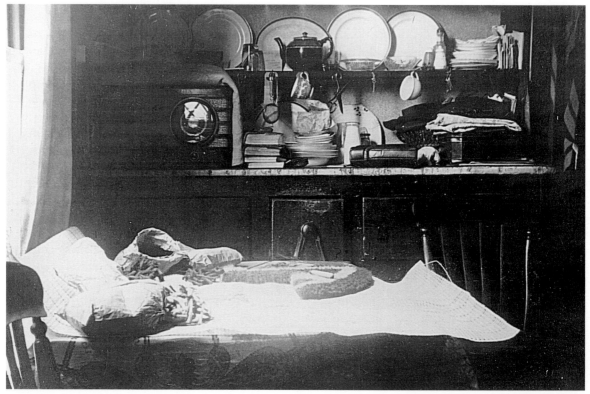

Making a rug on the kitchen table, about 1936.

chair, what you would call a nursing chair, I suppose. It was like a little dining wooden chair with sawn off legs and she used to sit alongside the radio... just in front of the fire... and listen there. (*Margaret Herridge, grew up in Stamshaw in the 1930s & '40s*)

For a shilling you could buy some meat, mince or beef cuttings or something like that. You could go to the greengrocers and get two pennyworth of mixed vegetables, and you could get some suet from the butchers. And mother used to make good old-fashioned stew with dumplings and potatoes, and that's the sort of thing we mostly had... except on a Friday when we had swordfish... it was lovely, and it was quite cheap, and it used to make quite a good meal for all the family... We could buy a rabbit for sixpence, take the skin off and sell it for ninepence,

so it never cost us anything really... and pigs' feet and pigs' trotters and all that sort of thing we used to make a meal of... tripe, onions, you don't know how lovely tripe is until you've tried it and it's cooked properly... [for Sunday] We used to be able to get a nice piece of beef for about 1s 6d... we used to get a nice piece of dripping, nice bit of dripping out of it for Sunday's tea. We always used to look forward to Sunday's tea with our dripping toast from the joint. And what was left on Monday, we'd have cold and if there was any left on Tuesday my mother minced it up in a mincing machine and we had a cottage pie... you could make a shilling go a long way in those days. (*Elsie Keld, born 1897, child in Fratton*)

Washday, we always had cold beef, left from Sunday, and bubble and squeak, which was all

the vegetables which weren't eaten on the Sunday, and rice pudding. It varied throughout the rest of the week, but Friday was always my favourite dinner because it was toasted cheese. Of course, the money had run out, but there was enough for a loaf of bread and a hunk of cheese, and so we would have toasted cheese for dinner. I used to think it was absolutely great to have toasted cheese for dinner, never realising that it was because it was the last of the week before the weekend.... On the other days, one of us used to go up to Fosters, on the corner of Curzon Howe Road, and get the meat in the mornings, because you got the meat fresh every day with whatever you were going to have for dinner... (*Anonymous, born Portsea, 1917*)

We also had a safe, a food safe, to put meat and stuff in because there was no refrigerator. In the summer we had little muslin things to go over the milk and they dipped into a bowl of water to keep the milk cool. And you always had to cover over the sugar because you had more flies in those days. The butter used to be in a glass dish which stood in an earthenware one and [we] put water in that to keep it cool. (*Vera Cole, grew up in Portsea and Milton in the 1910s–'20s*)

We went home [from school for lunch] because we lived quite near, only two or three minutes walk. My mother used to be a good cook, we had lots of home made things. Always home-made cakes and puddings. (*Doris*

Confectionery on sale in a shop in Lake Road, 1951.

Bealing, referring to Stamshaw in the 1930s–'40s)

Meals were always a family occasion. Cooked meals every evening, normally about half-past five. All persons were to be at the table, washed, cleaned, prepared... Casseroles, and things like shepherd's pie... meals that weren't expensive... There weren't any [convenience foods] no, oh no, I mean everything had to be freshly made... the meal time was the time when the family had that time together, what you would call now 'quality time', where you would discuss all the elements really. I mean what we all did and what we all achieved. It was very, for us it was a very important part of the day... then I was out playing... that was after

we had cleared up, mind you. That was the other rule of the kitchen, that after meals we took it in turns, and we had strict rotas on who was going to wash up, wipe up, put things away. (*Paul Barrett, child in Cosham, 1950s–'60s*)

We used to have home-cooked food, which was something like shepherd's pie, chicken, steak and kidney pie. I can remember eating from a tin of beans, but apart from that everything else was freshly prepared, because we didn't have a freezer and if you did have a freezer it was a very small compartment. So a lot of food was bought on the day... Occasionally we would have a sweet, something like home-made bread and butter pudding or

bread pudding, rhubarb and custard or crumble. All sorts of traditional English food really. I can't remember having a curry or spaghetti bolognese, it was all traditional British food. (*Graham Fletcher, grew up in Southsea 1960s–'70s*)

She [Mum] bought, like, frozen food, like pies and chips, and pizzas and veg, frozen veg. She used to buy a lot of frozen mixed veg, I used to hate it... She buys frozen curries now, and pot noodles because I come in late. (*Arran Stevens, child in the 1980s–'90s*)

Christmas was usually a very big dinner. We'd have gone to Mass, not eaten until we'd been to Mass. So we wouldn't have eaten

The Budd family celebrating Christmas, 1954.

since teatime the night before, 11.30, by that time be almost deliriously hungry, go back home and have big lunch. I remember one year Gran turned up trying to outdo my Mum with a big 22lb turkey and there were all sorts of fights with the taxi and we couldn't get it in the oven. We'd have a huge turkey, again Mum, not being a good cook – so lumpy gravy, and it would be appallingly cooked. (*Anonymous, child in Southsea in the 1960s*)

We don't have the traditional food [for Christmas] because quite a lot of my family are 'veggie' so we have an Indian take away. My dad goes out quite late Christmas Eve and buys it. We can just warm it up on Christmas day. It's a lot better than horrible turkey. (*Cathy Egan, child in the late 1980s–'90s*)

Housework and family routines

Until fairly recently, family life for most people meant a lot of time-consuming and arduous domestic tasks, most of which fell to mothers. Ironing without electricity involved heating up a pair of heavy irons on the stove, using them alternately. Before the introduction of labour-saving devices, a routine was essential to ensure that every aspect of domestic labour was covered on a regular basis. Without a bathroom and running hot water, bathing tended to be an

Mrs Taylor in an Oxford chair in her home on the Highbury estate, 1930s.

elaborate and drawn-out process as water would have to be carried in and heated in large pans on the stove or in a copper. For mothers, maintaining a family was very much a full-time job, although many had to find time for paid work as well. Children, especially older daughters, were expected to help out.

Mother used to work very hard and in fact I used to feel ashamed after I got married, because I can remember my mother had done every part of the housework before we had lunch at 12 o'clock. Dad came home at 12, the house was spotless. She then changed into another apron so she could do her needlework. And she always had a meal on the table and she worked extremely hard. Really hard. (*Anonymous, grew up in Buckland in the 1920s*)

A bathroom, no, that was a luxury that we had to wait years for I'm afraid. We had a big zinc bath hanging on the wall in the cellar and of course Friday nights, that was bath night mostly, Friday nights we would go down to the cellar and Mum would have the fire alight, this old Larbert range with pots and things on to heat the water and we would be bathed down in the cellar and of course we would have to have the same water, if two or three of us were bathed, it would probably have to be the same bath of water. I can't remember who went in first and then of course we would then have our hair washed and it was all done with Lifebuoy soap, the old red Lifebuoy soap which we all felt was very healthy in those days. (*Vera Cole, describing childhood in Portsea before 1916*)

We had a bath that we used to take into our house, and I think we boiled the water up. I suppose it was in these big kettles. You know, we just kept putting the water in and going and getting a

Eighteenth-century houses in White Hart Road. The man is Jimmy Sunshine, who saved a number of people from drowning in the nearby Camber.

bucketful or something out of the tap, and it wasn't very pleasant in the winter, because you know, I suspect I was one of them, but we couldn't turn the tap off, and then, of course, it would all get slippery there. So, many's the time, you know, we all got into trouble for leaving the tap on. (*Anonymous, born 1917, Portsea*)

We used to have to make the bath water go round a bit, so I think whoever was dirtiest had the last bath. I think probably weekends would have been the traditional time for baths. (*Paul Barratt, child 1950s–'60s*)

Monday was an all-day wash-day, in those days, there was no washing machines or anything like that. We did have a mangle, an old-fashioned mangle. I don't know what we would have done without the old mangle, and the copper where we used to boil the clothes and that sort of thing. (*Elsie Keld, born 1897*)

There was a landing at the top of the staircase where buckets of water were kept which Dad had to go right down to the cellar for. Down two other flights of stairs, one flight going down to the shop, the other flight going from the shop down to the cellar where there was just one tap, so you could imagine him coming up the stairs with probably only one bucket at a time. It was a huge bucket as far as I remember with fresh water and of course he [Dad] would have to empty any stale water that was used and go all that distance again because we only had the one lavatory which was also in the cellar. (*Vera Cole, describing life in Portsea before 1916*)

Facilities in a council house in Cosham in the 1920s were wonderful compared with those of a two-room house in a courtyard in Portsea.

Oh it was heaven compared with what we had had, you know, and they had just finished being built then, and we thought it was heavenly when we got that. Even

A photograph of a flat in Cosham, taken in 1957.

then, we didn't have hot water. There was a copper in the kitchen. It wasn't a copper built-in like my Gran had, but it was one that you could move out, you know, and boil all your washing up in it. It had a lid and had gas, which was, you know, really marvellous. (*Anonymous, born 1917*)

The advent of washing machines did not necessarily mean the end of hard physical work, as experience of this early post-war machine indicates.

They were actually called Jiffies... it did have a sort of gas heater underneath to heat the water in it... It had a sort of paddle inside, so when you put the lid down all you really did was paddle the clothes round. You know, instead of paddling it by hand, you were paddling it with this machine. The facility for heating the water in it was helpful. It had a little

mangle attached to it, and then you were able to take it out and push it through this little mangle... [it was] probably hard work when you think about it. You had to turn this thing. You couldn't go off and bake a cake whilst it was doing it. It was almost as hard work as doing it with the dollyboard thing – like they used to play skiffle on. At one time my mother used one of those. They used to have those and used to rub their clothes up and down those. It was the next step up from that. (*Ruth Williams, lived in Southsea, 1930s–'50s*)

I think the first washing machine we had was a Goblin and it had an enormous paddle wheel inside it and this thing used to thrash backwards and forwards. I don't think it did an awful lot of good for the clothes and it used to throw water in every direction. You couldn't put the lid on top to keep the water down because the

lid just used to vibrate off, so it was a case of you stood it on the lino in the middle of the room and just let it, sort of, thrash away to its own devices really. Then we got a very sophisticated one after that because it had an electric wringer on the top. Then I think we had a twin tub. (*David Reeves, referring to 1950s–'60s in Copnor*)

... we had two flat irons. You heated one [warmed on the gas stove] while you were using one and swapped over... my mother always had a trivet by the coal fire, she always had a kettle there, perhaps almost boiling, and she would finish it off on the gas. (*Doris Bealing, child in Stamshaw, 1930s–40s*)

Family entertainment and festivals

In the early 20th century mothers had little time for leisure. Even during the evenings there was patching and other sewing to be done. Fathers were often at the pub, as the very large number of public houses in the city before 1939 testifies. Nevertheless families did enjoy home-made entertainment, particularly on Sundays and at holiday times. Singing and various types of parlour games were common. In 1922 the BBC began broadcasting, and within a few years most homes had a radio. Television, although broadcasting from before

World War Two, did not acquire a mass audience until the mid-1950s. Visiting relatives was also a common weekend pastime.

May and Dick Hellyer with their son Geoffrey and May's mother Mabel Barber in the back garden of 10 Priory Crescent, Milton, 1958.

Mother was quite a good pianist and we all loved singing... [The piano] was in the front room. Used for piano practice. I was the only one who really took to the piano. Then it was used for parties and visitors. Our dining room was a very long room. We had one of those big mahogany tables that you had a big key to wind it up and down to put leaves in or take leaves out... we would sit about 30 friends and relations there for the New Year's Eve party. Christmas Day was children's day when my cousins used to come round but that was a much smaller affair... we used to have these absolutely gorgeous parties and I graduated from helping mother prepare, to then going to lay the table and going up to bed with a tray of little

goodies, and I gradually was allowed to stay up later and later and in the end I was there all the time... They really were wonderful evenings. Musical always, lots of games. Dad was very good at games. (*Joy Hobbs, child 1920s–'30s*)

We used to sing a lot... we used to sit round the fire, always used to sit round the fire and sing... my dad would have me on his knee... I was sent to a man my dad worked with. He was a recorder in the dockyard and he taught music lessons... if anyone ever asked I said "No, I never had any theory", but nevertheless he taught me to play and even entered me into the festival once at the Guildhall. (*Vera Cole, child 1910s–'20s*)

Most children played out in the street.

No, my mother wouldn't allow that. No. Nice children didn't play out in the street! That's why, looking back, she must have been the most awful snob... Sunday afternoons she would walk us up through Victoria Park in our Sunday best, and I always had an Easter bonnet each Easter, when everybody paraded their Easter bonnets. There was a bandstand up there then. We used to go and sit and listen to the band. That was nice. Victoria Park has always played a big part, really, in my life. (*Anonymous, born 1917 in Portsea*)

There weren't that many cars around in those days and so you had the freedom to play in the street because, certainly during the time I was growing up, I probably could have counted on one hand the number of cars that were actually owned by anyone

Len Robinson and friends, Landport, about 1925.

in the area... There were a number of horse and carts around and a number of old buildings which had horses in, and a lot of kids would get to know the various people who operated horses. And Kneller was a well known trader who used to sell fruit and veg around the houses from the back of a horse and cart, and many's a kid supposedly learnt to ride on the back of Kneller's horse. The fact that it was always hitched to a trailer didn't seem to deflect from the fact that we were all Roy Rogers or Gene Autrey or whoever it was at the time. (*Mike Hancock, grew up in Portsea in the 1940s & '50s*)

When a father was often not working, simple gifts were very much appreciated.

I think we got a slate and a piece of chalk [for Christmas], which we thought was lovely... I know we used to have a sock with an apple, an orange and few nuts in, which we thought was really something. I remember that sometimes we had, perhaps, some paints or a little book. I can't remember anything extra big, but we thought that was lovely when we had that. (*Anonymous, born 1917 in Portsea*)

Dad used to do the fireworks. He used to put one of the airers... and he used to pin them all on there. Grandad used to make us a guy. So we used to have Guy Fawkes' night in the garden. When you look back on it now and think what a tiny garden it was, it's amazing really, because

Louise and her birthday cake, 1990s.

everybody along there was doing the same thing, that there weren't more accidents. We were right on top of each other. (*Anonymous, child in Portsea, 1920s*)

Yes, that [radio] was our main source of entertainment. I can remember Saturday nights, we would have our bath and then be allowed to sit up later and listen to things on the radio. And there was Children's Hour, of course, which we liked. We didn't have an ordinary radio because the house still had gaslight at that time, so we had what they called 'Radio Relay' which came in to the house like a telephone system... You had just two switches for whatever programme you wanted and it came straight into your

loudspeaker. (*Doris Bealing, child 1930s–'40s*)

Radio was the main source of entertainment. I can remember as a child that there were a couple of things that I was allowed to stay up late and listen to. One was *Journey Into Space* and the other one was *Dick Barton* and that was the two evenings of the week that I was allowed to stay up late. I always had to have my bath and put my pyjamas on before it started, so as soon as it had finished I was off to bed.

This respondent also recalls very vividly the day the family acquired its first television set.

I think I was about 12, 13 when

we had our first television set. My father bought one second-hand from a local junk shop and I'll always remember this television set. It was wheeled into the living room. It was a walnut console cabinet with two open doors at the front. Beautiful piece of furniture. And so the plug was put on and the aerial was put in the back and the doors were opened ceremoniously and the first thing I ever saw on television was a circus. Unfortunately, being second-hand and not in too good a condition the picture kept rolling round and whatever Dad did, struggling around the back of the set with lots of grunts and groans and

"I'm sure it'll be all right in a minute", the picture was either going up or down. (*David Reeves, child in mid-1950s Copnor*)

Neighbourhood and community life

A common recollection is that each district was more friendly in the early 20th century than later.

I think people here looked out for one another, the neighbours were much more friendly. Everybody knew everybody else along the street. I remember lots of names of the families, and they had grown up together. People didn't

move about so much and there was three or four generations in one road. (*Doris Bealing, describing Stamshaw in 1930s–'40s*)

I came from a very large extended family so living close to me there were anything from, I think, 20 to 30 cousins and what-have-you at one time. And so there was always somebody in the street who was related to you, or round about, and so it was, particularly in Portsea where there were a large number of members of the family living at one time, certainly during the period from the late '40s to the late '50s. And so there was

Mrs Ada Harper at her gate in Montgomerie Road, about 1964.

always someone close at hand. (*Michael Hancock, born in Portsea*)

Charles Street in particular, on a summer's evening, you could walk through Charles Street and you would find people sitting on their window ledges outside, sort of community together. More than that, there was a community spirit in the sense that, although some of them used to fight like tomcats, if any one of them was in any real serious trouble, they all rallied round... I've got memories of street wars between certain families that would clash, and if there was a street war between certain families, nobody put their head outside the door or else they might have been hit with a brick. (*Mr Stevens, a butcher in Landport before World War Two*)

You travel more now. People have cars, and you go all over the place, but people stuck in their own little areas in those days. We lived off Somers Road, we shopped in Somers Road. There were no supermarkets, so you shopped locally, and practically every area had its own little Co-op and its little Co-op butchers, and there wasn't the big stores like you have now. I doubt if I even knew Charlotte Street existed in those days, because it wasn't our area. My mother used to go up Albert Road sometimes just to go somewhere. (*Ruth Williams, referring to Southsea in the 1930s & '40s*)

There are three Bangladeshi food shops in Portsmouth – Somers

The MA Food Cash and Carry, a self-service supermarket, Kingston Road, 2002.

Road, Elm Grove and Palmerston Road, where we do our shopping. (*Karim Choudury, member of Portsmouth's Bangladeshi community, recorded 1998*)

In our road, it wasn't very long, and we used to live down one end, right near the school gates... and up the other end – they were supposed to be the elite up there. Oh it used to be so funny. Their children weren't allowed to come out and play... they wouldn't mix with us, we were the lower end. We used to laugh at it though. We never let it interfere with our enjoyment... I can still see some of them walking past now, with their noses in the air. (*Anonymous, born 1912*)

People began to go within themselves and you weren't friendly like you were during the war. No... there was a difference. And the more stuff that came into the shops, the more you could buy, the more people

grabbed. In a way, I suppose it was because they were starved, not starved like material, furniture and all that. They had been starved of the choice. But now there was a choice so people were like, you know, keep up with the Jones's, and the grabbing. (*Cynthia Bartlett, born in the early 1930s*)

But there is still neighbourliness today.

I am very long time in this country. I know a bit more than the others. For any help that they need, if they are stuck with an official form or to go to the bank, I can go down with them. (*Karim Choudury, came to Portsmouth in 1972 from Bangladesh*)

Father was also a member of the civil service sports club and that was quite good 'cos it meant that they would have to take me along. It was well organised... there were three elements to the

Commercial Road, pedestrianised in the 1970s. For many, shopping has become a leisure activity, not merely a necessary task.

club, there was bowling, which my father was interested in, there was tennis and there was a cricket team... they would play a game of cricket or a game of tennis in the afternoon, then they would have a dance in the evenings. So that was an excuse for me to stay. Because it was a club I could go in there, and there were other children... Also it gave me my first insight into coach travel because they used to play against, like, organisations from places like Basingstoke, Bournemouth, Southampton, Weybridge. Those four places they used to go to every year and that was quite exciting because you would go to the North End and three coaches would turn up,

one for each team, and we would go off and that was... real adventure that was, went to see all these far-flung places. (*Terry Chase, child 1950s–'60s*)

We used to go to a place called Cooper's garages which is where Wimbledon Park is today. When I first went there it was fenced off to the public. It was an old skating rink, and we used to all play down there. And Southsea's quite a high-built area and at that time there was very little park areas for children to go and play. So I can remember that there came a time that the parents of that area, the Wimbledon Park area, actually formed a committee and

pressurised the council to turn that place into a park. And I can remember in the summer we would have something like a barbecue and with hot dogs, and whatever, and we would have firework displays and a big bonfire there, and everybody was encouraged to participate. So it was quite a good community spirit there, and eventually... I can actually remember some guy, some councillor came down to the park, when we were playing, and having a discussion with the mums. I remember him saying that we want to do this and we want to do that and, to their credit, it did actually happen in the '70s. They did demolish the old skating rink and put a football pitch there, and they put children's slides, that kind of thing. The only down factor of it was as soon as they did have all these nice amenities 15 and 16-year-old kids just came in and wrecked them. I can remember them actually doing it, seeing them doing it... It was quite upsetting at the time. (*Graham Fletcher, talking about the early 1970s*)

I keep myself to myself. I mean I do have good neighbours either side of me and down-the-way, but apart from that I do keep myself to myself, because the young children round here have no respect for anything. They shout at you when you go round the shops and when – before I had the telephone I used to go round to the telephone box, and that was horrendous, really horrendous... But now it is the bikes. You go walking down the road and you turn a corner and there is a bike coming at you... I'm not as nimble as I used to be and can't always get out of the way....You shout at them because you are so... "What are you doing that for!" sort of thing, and all you get is abuse. "Get off the road! Why are you still alive?", more-or-less. Charming! But I'm afraid it is today's society that is like that. (*Anonymous, Buckland*)

Many Portsmouth families experienced poverty.

We could take a cup over to the little shop and buy a pennyworth of mixed pickle or two-pennyworth of onions, you know, in a cup. Or some beetroot, you know, for a penny and two pence which would make our Monday's dinner up. Or you could take your cup over there and he would give you three or four-pennyworth of jam out of a big stone jar. You lived like that, you lived from day-to-day... in those days if you pleaded poverty, it was a plea too. There was a

Street parties, like this in Landport for George V's silver jubilee in 1935, demonstrated neighbourliness among even the poorest communities.

brotherhood place down in Arundel Street and you could go there and after you'd pleaded, and you had nothing to sell, they'd let you have a pair of boots for one of the boys or something like that. Or if you wanted groceries you'd come down to, was it St Michael's Road round here [the offices of the Board of Guardians], and "Have you got a piano to sell?" And all that sort of thing, see what you had... before they'd let you have a voucher for 6s to buy a week's groceries. (*Elsie Keld, born 1897*)

Religion played an important part in many citizens' lives, but not everyone was religious.

Dad wasn't. Mum was until she had all the children and she couldn't make it [to church]. But she belonged to the Mother's Union at the church – St Cuthbert's at Copnor used to have monthly socials and whist drives and that, which Mum and Dad always went to, and there were games for the children. (*Joy Hobbs, remembering the 1920s & '30s*)

Right next to the school we had the church, St Matthew's Church, and I joined the church, and joined a guild that friends of mine went to. We had a

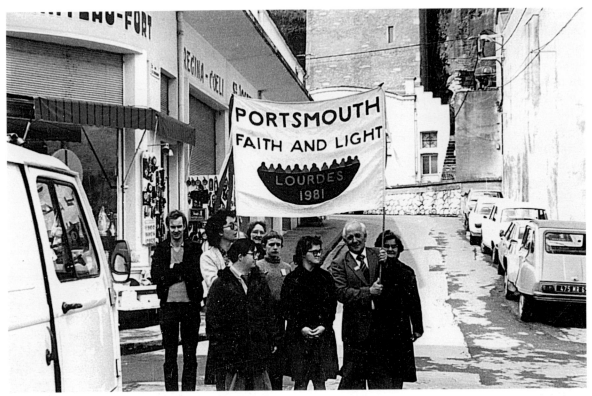

A group of Portsmouth Roman Catholics on pilgrimage to Lourdes, 1981.

glorious time round there, we loved going to church... and there were lots of hymns now I like. In fact my favourite hymn as a child was *All Things Bright and Beautiful* and I told my daughter that's the hymn I want... at my funeral. (*Vera Cole, child in Portsea, Southsea and Milton, 1910s–'20s*)

When I was about 13 I joined the church choir, and started going to church on a regular basis, and then was confirmed. And I went to church regularly for about six or seven years. And I became quite sort of disillusioned with it, so I stopped going. That was at Warren Park, St Clare's in Warren Park. (*Gail Stewart-Bye, referring to late 1970s Bedhampton*)

I can remember at a very early age my Mum and Dad encouraged me to go to a Methodist hall in Inglis Road. I can remember going there and there used to be a Sunday School and we used to sing songs and all that. I wasn't really interested in that, but they had a very good youth club there. (*Graham Fletcher, referring to 1970s Southsea*)

In Portsmouth I go to the Mosque every Friday to pray. In Bangladesh it would be five times a day, but the Mosque is too far away... Friday is our special day... and we have a special month of fasting, Ramadan, when we can only eat between sunset and sunrise. It's very hard. (*Karim Choudury, Muslim, originally from Bangladesh*)

At prayer in Portsmouth's new mosque, 2002.

Newcomers to the city usually settled easily, but there were still areas of tension. This respondent's father was one of the many

A Devonian Society dinner dance, February 1953. The society organised social functions for Portsmouth people who had, or whose relations had, migrated from Devon.

who came from Wales, while she herself spent time there as an evacuee.

My father had a Welsh accent all his life, because he came up here as an adult, but mine disappeared very quickly. Which was just as well, because the teachers quite liked that and they wanted to hear that as well, you know. It's funny, children don't like to be different. (*Ruth Williams, child in Southsea, 1940s–'50s*)

Ties with home were often strong and endured over many years.

One of the things about being Cornishmen up here was that we were aliens. You know, we would go back and bring back clotted cream and things like that you couldn't get locally. So whenever we went down to Cornwall, which we did quite frequently, we would then bring back food parcels, which would then keep us for several months. (*Neville Penter, came to Portsmouth from Liskeard, 1956*)

This respondent grew up in a family of Italian immigrants who set up a café and ice cream business in Guildhall Square in the 1930s.

We had our holiday in the winter, we'd go back to Italy... on a Sunday we used to have to have lunch with my grandfather at 12 o'clock and then go and have another lunch with my other grandfather at one o'clock, otherwise they would both get upset. So on Sunday it was two lunches, they made you drink wine, so it was quite a feat. (*Lidia Briano, young in the 1940s & '50s*)

PORTSMOUTH LIVES:

FROM CHILDHOOD TO ADULTHOOD IN 20TH-CENTURY PORTSMOUTH

Portsea Free School photographed outside St George's Church, 1920.

Gail Stewart-Bye and Ligia Kašanin

Whip and top, diabolo, skipping and snap, card games, ludo, snakes and ladders, tiddly winks.
(Mrs G. Chase, child in the 1920s)

Introduction

The many diverse experiences of growing up in Portsmouth during the 20th century reflect the constantly changing nature of society throughout the period, as well as more specific local changes. For urban children during the first half of the century, local streets, with virtually no traffic, constituted their playground and provided the arena for a wide variety of games. The inexorable growth of motor traffic has rendered street play a largely forgotten pleasure for today's children, who instead enjoy indoor, technologically-advanced activities and organised play schemes, both unimaginable in earlier times.

Few working-class children in Portsmouth received any formal education before 1870. The exceptions were those attending the Beneficial School in Portsea, established in 1754 and still operational over 200 years later, and the Royal Dockyard School, opened by the Admiralty in 1843 to cater for dockyard entrance. With the 1870 Education Act, however, substantial developments were made to the city's educational provision, and by 1903 almost 31,000 children attended 36 elementary and one 'higher grade' schools. The 20th century witnessed still more dramatic changes in concepts of education, perhaps most notably visible in the introduction of free state secondary schools for all children after the Education Act of 1944. This heralded further innovation in the development of three different types of education, based upon children's individual needs and abilities: grammar, modern, and technical schools were born. 'Special' schools were also provided for children with extra physical or intellectual needs.

For many young people in the earlier part of the century, learning about sex and childbirth were synonymous with marriage. However, later recollections reflect a more relaxed attitude, with children learning the 'facts of life' at a very young age. For those getting married, the traditional wedding remained very popular throughout the period, although during World War Two, when food and clothes were hard to come by, couples wanting the traditional trimmings were forced to become very inventive. Before the creation of the National Health Service in

1948, all medical care had to be paid for. The development of free healthcare, together with an improved diet has meant that few people now come into contact, much less suffer, from once common diseases such as mumps, measles, scarlet fever and diphtheria. It now seems inconceivable that all of Portsmouth's schools were forced to close because of the effects of the 1919 'flu epidemic.

Play

Sophisticated toys seldom feature in early childhood recollections; in 1920s Portsea for example, John Slade remembered using a pig's bladder from the local slaughterhouse to kick around as a football. A piece of chalk with which to mark out the squares of hopscotch or a length of rope for skipping were often the only ingredients necessary for a good time, and games such as these have endured into the 21st century.

... we used to play in the street... we had a long skipping rope that used to stretch across the road and two girls, one each end, turning it, and we'd run in and

Children in Landport, about 1930.

skip and come round again, no traffic... Hopscotch, cherry-bobs we used to play. We used to get – ask the man in the shop to give us an empty Woodbine box... and we used to punch holes in the top and we used to get cherry stones and we used to sit on the kerb and pitch the cherry stones and see how many we could get in the holes in the box, and that used to keep us quiet. (*Elsie Keld, child, early 1900s*)

We used to play in the street, mostly. We used to have marbles and cards, and buttons, and skipping; we used to enjoy it really. In summer, we used to take our lemonade and all that type of thing – make our own lemonade up – and sandwiches... and off we used to go over the hill. We used to pick bluebells and come back with bundles of bluebells, and they would all be dead by the time we got home. We used to go on the tram. (*Constance Godding, child, 1920s–'30s*)

Opposite our house there was a garage which made an ideal goal and we used to play football, one in goal, kicking into the goal. The policeman used to come round the corner and stop us, and he used to tell us off and said [we] mustn't play ball in the streets. So we used to pack up playing football and as soon as he disappeared round the corner, we used to start again! 'Course he went round the square and caught us again on the way back! (*Mr E. Chase, child, 1920s–'30s*)

Our childhood days were a dream

really. I mean, we had no money, we used to play what they call marbles now. We called them glass alleys, my younger sister and I. We used to play them in the gutter like, with boys, you know, and win all their lovely marbles, beautiful things. (*Cynthia Bartlett, child, 1930s–'40s*)

Paul Barratt, about 1960.

We played out in the street, most commonly football and French cricket... you used, like, a tennis racquet as a cricket bat. All the children in the street would all be out there playing... [in] Invergordon Avenue. Our house was directly opposite a junction, which gave us a bit more room to play in, which was ideal for this French cricket game. Nobody complained about children playing in the road, it was safe. (*Paul Barratt, child, 1950s–'60s*)

Even sewing dolls' clothes was done on the roadside...

...we'd go round to Staunton Street... and there was a lady used to be there, and we used to buy ha'porth of patchwork quilt, little bits of rags and all that. And we'd come back and we'd sit

on the pavement and we'd have our little dolls, and needle and cotton, and we used to make, which we thought was nice, used to make little things for the dolls and all that. (*Emma Smith, child in Landport, 1920s*)

A favoured activity since the first warships came to Portsmouth, 'mudlarking' at Portsea Hard continued to be popular throughout the first half of the 20th century, and featured in accounts from the early 1900s until the 1950s. Other trends, such as cigarette card collecting and games also endured over several decades:

Cigarette cards were very popular, and there were flicks... flicks was when they put three cigarette cards up against the wall and you stood or kneeled back by the edge of the kerb – and you flicked yours to try and knock the others down... that was a great thing, cigarette cards. (*Keswick Withy, child, 1920s*)

We used to play a form of snap with cigarette cards, because you always ended up with doubles of cigarette cards, and we used to have a set that we would stick in a book and then we would have a set that we would play with. (*David Reeves, child, 1940s–'50s*)

The 1950s 'culture of affluence', following the austerity of the previous two decades enabled many children to benefit from toys and games their parents would not have dreamed of owning.

Brian and Christine Moon, 1958-9.

I can remember my parents buying me a cowboy outfit, which was not bad. It wasn't as good as some of my contemporaries, because you could buy a super-duper cowboy outfit or a basic one. I remember wanting it for about, at least, a year, and when I got it I was too sort of – I didn't want to go out in it – I felt embarrassed... Other lads had Davy Crockett outfits and they were all the rage in 1957–58 with a long hat... a plastic rifle. Not many children had the Indian outfits. It seemed to me, if you had an Indian outfit you were the enemy. The following year... spaceships... that was all the rage with silver suits. (*Ernest Aspey, child, 1950s*)

And play often took place in the home rather than in the street outside.

I can remember having lead soldiers, not very many. Mostly cowboys and Indians, of course, were the in-thing in my day, and I can remember having models of cowboys and Indians that I used to play with on the carpet in front of the fire. One of my greatest acquisitions was a covered wagon. I think that was probably one of the top toys in the Dinky range and that was really great. (*David Reeves, child, 1940s–'50s*)

Later still, those street games of earlier days were now

played in the school playground.

In school we played five-jacks and marbles, and hopscotch, skipping; two-balls and hand-clapping we did a lot of, and also those balls, you had two little balls on a string and you used to whack them up and down... but I was always scared of them, I was scared of getting hurt. (*Gail Stewart-Bye, child, 1970s*)

But the technological advances of the late 20th century surely had more impact on play than any other development:

I usually play on my Play Station

Stefan and Anton Kašanin.

with my brother. I play car-racing games, fighting games and 'platform' games; they've got levels and they've got puzzles for each level and you've got to solve the puzzle. Sometimes I play with Lego, and my brother and I build cars and bases with guns, and we call it our Lego Force. (*Stefan Kašanin, child, 1990s*)

School

Before 1944, only those whose parents could afford to pay for secondary education were able to continue their schooling beyond the age of 14.

I always wanted to go to the, well, it's the grammar school now. I can remember on Fridays, when this homework was given out [to the girls going on to secondary school], we had silent reading, it was very much an us

and them situation... I was always envious of the girls who went to the secondary school... you either paid, or you didn't go. (*Anonymous schoolgirl, 1910s*)

The structure of school life, the equipment provided and the subjects studied inevitably altered throughout

the period, as changes in ideas about education and in educational policy made themselves felt, and more capital was invested in schools. The emphasis in the first half of the century was on practical tasks, together with the 'three Rs'. It is perhaps the first memories of school life that linger longest, frequently associated with a certain smell which will always have connotations of school.

I can remember my first day there. I would be about four and a half when I started... The teacher's name was... Miss Fevre, I believe it was. A very tall person with swept-back black hair, a bun at the back and a long black dress. And I can still smell that classroom now – the disinfectant and soap on the woodblock floor. (*Ken Freemantle, schoolboy, 1920s*)

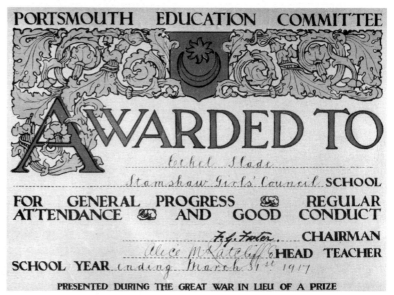

PORTSMOUTH EDUCATION COMMITTEE

AWARDED TO

Ethel Slade

Stamshaw Girls' Council SCHOOL

FOR GENERAL PROGRESS & REGULAR ATTENDANCE & AND GOOD CONDUCT

L. G. Foster CHAIRMAN

Alice M. Ratcliffe HEAD TEACHER

SCHOOL YEAR *ending March 31st 1917*

PRESENTED DURING THE GREAT WAR IN LIEU OF A PRIZE

Certificate in lieu of a prize awarded to Ethel Slade during World War One.

He used to sit up on a sort of desk like a lectern, the master did, and alongside him was a big open coal fire, we never had no central heating or nothing like that in there. And... Mr Street, who was the caretaker, he used to come round three times a morning, in the winter, and stoke up the fire, make up the fire, and we used to have free milk, which was one third of a pint and those who wanted warm milk, that was put round the fireplace for when the playtime came. (*John Slade, schoolboy, 1920s*)

When I was 11 I could knit a man's sock and turn the heel and all that through learning at school. And I remember when I

first went into the big girls' school, we were asked to do a buttonhole, and I won sixpence for doing the best buttonhole... Oh, arithmetic, writing, essays, dictation, oh all sorts of things, how to write, how to write properly, how to sit properly at your desk and write, not like they do nowadays. You sat properly and you wrote, and when you wrote you wrote with your thin strokes up, thick strokes down and so on. Your writing was beautiful [in] those days. (*Elsie Keld, schoolgirl, early 1900s*)

... every morning, after you had said your prayers, which was your religious instruction, in the class that I was in, you would,

first of all, have 20 mental arithmetic questions and, of course, you got good and bad marks for that dependent upon how many of those you had right. After that, we always had to have a word every day, and the teacher would give us a word, and then, by the next morning, you had to have found out what it meant from the dictionary and also used it in a sentence to show that you understood what it meant. That was how we got our vocabulary. (*Anonymous schoolgirl, 1920s*)

There was a line of good handwriting and you copied it on the line underneath, and writing was done by nib pens and ink.

Mr Gonin's Class, Stamshaw Junior School, about 1930.

We had a desk with an inkwell in it, it was a china inkwell and the ink was made up out of Stephenson's powdered ink. If you were a silly boy and you volunteered for ink monitor, once a month you'd have to take all the ink bottles, take them out and put them in the sink and wash them all out, and your hands used to get covered in ink... (*Keswick Withy, schoolboy, 1930s*)

When I was in the infants' school we had chalkboards and we also had sand trays, which you wrote in with your finger in the sand. But when we were in the junior school we had pencils but they were just plain wood, what you called utility ones. (*Doris Bealing, Schoolgirl, 1930s–'40s*)

In the 1960s and 1970s technological developments, together with new ideas about learning resulted in some innovative forms of teaching, which left respondents with some interesting recollections:

Physics was very interesting. Mr Seeley was the physics teacher, and this was back in the late '60s... and he was telling us about Quantum Physics which were literally just coming out of the press... he was so up-to-speed it was incredible, and it was wonderful, and you could have, you could understand it. I mean I have a picture in my mind of Newtonian Physics... and I have a picture in my mind of Quantum Physics, that that guy put in my head, and its still vivid, its still

useful, its still applicable. (*Neville Penter, schoolboy, 1960s*)

Mr Green... he actually made up a song about the class, which was quite interesting, plus he actually used everybody's name, he was a clever man. He sat in class one day, with his guitar, and he actually sang the whole of this song, at the register and as he sang your name you had to say 'Sir'. It was really weird. (*Keith Ayres, schoolboy, 1960s*)

School uniform was not commonly worn in state schools until after World War Two; however at the beginning of the century merely possessing a good pair of shoes was for some children an unaffordable luxury.

I had no boots or shoes; I used to walk to school with bare feet. And then they brought out

Goodwill Boots, which were stamped so you couldn't pawn them you know... (basically we only wore shoes or boots on Sundays when we had our best clothes on)... and you mustn't be caught skipping with them or hopping with them because if anybody caught you they said "We paid for that and you're wearing them out!" (*John Slade, schoolboy, 1920s*)

By contrast this account of school life just a few years later is an indication of the dramatic gulf existing between Portsmouth families living just a few miles apart.

I went in 1934 and the school opened in 1932... brown tunics and fawn blouses. But they were square necked and that was quite an innovation because we didn't have collars and ties. Brown stockings, brown blazers, brown topcoats and first of all we had

Learning through play, St George's School Portsea at its opening in 1962. (By courtesy of *The News*)

brown velour hats but after the first year, they went out and we had berets which was much more sensible... in the summer we had blue and green cotton frocks. (*Joy Hobbs, schoolgirl, 1930s*)

In those days a lot of parents couldn't afford for their children to go to grammar school... that was because at grammar school they had to have uniforms, there was no optional attitude to uniforms, and the uniform requirements were fairly demanding... children who had passed or were quite capable of passing were actually not encouraged to go on to grammar school because their parents couldn't afford to do it. (*Sue Spencer, schoolgirl, 1950s*)

School uniform was worn with pride in the 1940s; but by 1960 pupils had found some interesting ways of saying a final goodbye to an unwanted encumbrance.

We had a badge on the pocket of the blazer, and you had to buy the blazer in Lake Road. Bakers, I think, was the name of the shop, if I remember rightly. With your grey trousers and your shirt and your pully. And you bought the badge from school and your parents had to sew the badge on. And when you got made a prefect you had the ribbons on your hat, a little braiding... And the hats were black with yellow, a sort of cord sewn to them if you'd 'earned your rent' sort of thing. We were all very proud of our uniforms. (*Brian Gray, schoolboy, 1940s*)

Technical High School was black, charcoal grey jacket with a badge on the pocket, and we had to wear caps. We were the only school in Portsmouth that had to wear caps and detention if you didn't wear a cap on a bus and things like that... when we left school the ritual was to cut your tie in half and burn your cap, which was quite fun. (*Neville Penter, schoolboy, 1960s*)

Memories of school life were not always recalled with such pleasure however, and teachers were, sadly, often remembered with something less than affection, or even respect. Prior to the abolition of corporal punishment in the 1980s, interviewees frequently recollect harsh regimes and discipline policies that included the use of the cane or slipper, particularly for boys. The manner in which these physical punishments were administered can in some cases only be described as malevolent.

You had Assembly, you had to be

Neville Penter in his new uniform for the Technical High School, 1965.

there... at nine o'clock, and if you wasn't there a minute before that door was opened... you got the cane... I was late once... and we got there I can remember and the door was, someone just shut the door as we was there, but we weren't allowed in, we weren't allowed in. (*Emma Smith, schoolgirl, 1920s*)

When I hear of the terrible schools and all the criticism of teachers and so on and the behaviour in schools, I can only say they should have seen schools in those days. Some of the classes were a complete riot because the masters couldn't control the children. I have seen on several occasions stand-up fights between boys and teachers. And yet we were told we used to get the highest results in the south of England. I only wonder what some of the others got. (*Stanley Riddell, schoolboy, 1920s–'30s*)

The head teacher, he was one of the 'old school'. He used the cane sparingly and he was one of the real old gentlemen of schooling. But some of the other teachers were pretty rough and ready, and of course, one of things that was really bad was that if you were unable to do the work, they didn't put it down to their teaching, they put it down to your not paying attention, and to get walloped over the top of the head with a heavy book wasn't uncommon, and the use of the slipper and the cane in the classrooms was quite prevalent... I mean, I can remember having the slipper and the cane. I can

Country dancing at Court Lane School, 1963, a common method of giving primary school children exercise.

remember being so ashamed of having the cane and, sort of hiding upstairs in my bedroom, and my hand throbbing and swelling up and not wanting to tell anybody. (*David Reeves, schoolboy, 1950s*)

We had several teachers who left the school in disgrace for sex offences, I mean, they obviously made quite an impression. My first-year tutor made an incredible impression, he was like a sadist... really violent and so on, he used to hit us with a slipper twice a day, there used to be two sessions in the morning and after lunch... It was a sort of ritualised beating... basically every day he'd hit me, you know, bend over, make me bend over in the class and hit me, but he

would with... a good 20-25 per cent of the class he would do this every day. I felt victimised... definitely he'd hit the more working class kids... but it was just part of the arbitrariness of life really. (*Anonymous schoolboy, 1970s*)

About half of them wore gowns. On any special days they would wear mortarboards and I don't know what you call them, all the coloured shawl-like things, otherwise it was just black gowns. Though one master used to turn up in the summer in shorts, and some of them were really a disgrace. One of them had his glasses tied up with a bit of string and sticky tape, and some of the others looked as though their clothes could have

done with a good clean. They were not at all a neat and tidy looking lot. (*Stanley Riddell, schoolboy, 1920s–'30s*)

I do think that the schooling, the teachers in Southern Grammar School were pretty useless on the whole. The older teachers were strict and the pupils were afraid of them, but the younger ones were just a joke. It was the 1970s, and I suppose the whole climate was you know, freedom of this, and freedom of that, let children express themselves... We had absolutely no respect for most of the teachers, they had no authority, no personality; they weren't stimulating, just totally uninspiring. Perhaps our expectations were too high. (*Ligia Kašanin, schoolgirl, 1970s*)

Obviously there were certain teachers who couldn't control a class, some children would play on that and just disrupt the class for the whole lesson. And there were quite a few children who would backchat or just generally muck around, and the discipline was not really that strict... there wasn't a lot of violence, hardly any, just really kids clowning around... Which was quite annoying for those people who wanted to do well, and who wanted to get on at school... you didn't want to appear to be a goody-goody at school, so there was always an element of wanting to do well and wanting to stay in with the other children. (*Gail Stewart-Bye, schoolgirl, Broomfield, 1970s*)

By the 1980s, the concept of discipline and punishment had changed considerably.

They were quite strict... but I remember one time when I had done something wrong, we had a new headmistress, [I] can't remember her name, and she called me into her office, [and] because I was in there so often she sat me down and gave me a Milky Way, and said, "Now, we'll just talk about this shall we?" (*Arran Stevens, schoolboy, 1980s*)

If we forget our homework more than three times we get a lunchtime detention, if we forget it another time or we don't attend the lunchtime detention we get an after-school detention. If we

muck about in class a lot of the time we get put on 'pink slip', which means that after every lesson the teacher writes down how we have behaved in the lesson; if we don't behave we get an after-school detention. Once my whole form was put on 'pink slip' and at least five people were given an after-school detention. (*Anton Kašanin, schoolboy, 1990s*)

Some respondents did actually enjoy school:

It was lovely. They weren't like they are now. The teachers were lovely. They were a lot older than they are today, but we had to respect them. Not call them Joan and June, and all this type of

A cricket team at St Helen's College, Southsea, about 1932.

thing. We had to call them 'Miss' all the time. They were lovely. I had a lovely childhood, really. We didn't have a uniform then, because we couldn't afford it. School was lovely, really. (*Constance Godding, schoolgirl, 1930s*)

In 1975 the tripartite system was abolished in Portsmouth, making way for a more egalitarian form of education in the shape of comprehensive schooling. The 11-plus was eliminated. Many respondents remembered keenly the pernicious effects of failing these controversial examinations.

Devastated, in a word, when I got the results, because... you all would like to go to the grammar school because we all knew... it had been preached by our teachers... this was the future. The 11-plus was the most

Caitlin. Sweatshirts and polo shirts were uniform in many schools in the 1990s.

important day of your life... and when you went to Hilsea you thought the world had fallen out... You adjust, but you knew that you were amongst the masses rather than the elite... Eventually after about two years, they formed a GCE group at Hilsea Modern, and I became part of that. And that was formed from boys from all over Portsmouth, because the 11-plus was so devastating... They had some bright lads there who should have passed the 11-plus but failed for a variety of reasons. I think basically this is how the comprehensive system started. They suddenly realised that this 11-plus was so decisive and so devastating. (*Ernest Aspey, schoolboy, 1950s*)

I think they [my parents] were disappointed, they were too polite to say, I mean you had the sort of phrases like "Well, never mind, it's not the end of the world" etc, etc, but you did tend to feel that it was... The bright went to grammar school, and you were considered a cut above the rest, you had a smart uniform and a tie. If you went to the technical school you also wore a smart uniform and tie, but you were slightly looked down on compared to a grammar school boy. If you went to the modern school, it's an exaggeration to say you didn't have a uniform at all, but you tended to be in the lower echelons of society, if I may say, and you felt pretty bad about that – it was a sense of failure, definitely. (*Terry Chase, schoolboy, 1950s*)

Two respondents from the amalgamated Priory School in Fawcett Road recalled how they felt about 'going comprehensive'.

... I can remember initially, we said we didn't want to leave, we wanted to stay on that site... We had quite an identity, it was good to be at Southsea Modern. I can remember a lot didn't want to go up there because a lot of Southern Grammar School girls we thought of as snobs, and also I think deep down we all knew that intellectually they were quite superior to what we were, and we didn't enjoy that. (*Graham Fletcher, schoolboy, 1970s*)

We went comprehensive and we had what seemed to me, a lot of very rough children. They were not as well educated as we were because we were grammar school children, and they were rough. They swore, and they smoked, we did smoke, but we were much more circumspect about it – they were much more overt. They were rude, they were loud and they were scruffy. My first impression of them was that we had been invaded by these very loud, scruffy people, probably that's very unfair. (*Ligia Kašanin, schoolgirl, 1970s*)

Moreover, despite the introduction of the comprehensive system, an egalitarian education was not a universal experience.

There was, what we always referred to as, an elite group at school who were always known

A Victorian school stands out above the houses in this view across Buckland during redevelopment in the late 1960s.

as the real boffins, you know, they were like a little section apart from us, who were destined to do well, which really annoyed me, because I felt that the rest of us were just cast aside and categorised without really being given a chance. And I think that is part of the reason why it took me so long to get to do my degree, because of their attitude. (*Gail Stewart-Bye, schoolgirl, late 1970s*)

Several interviewees recalled some of their own and other pupils' misdemeanours.

We got hold of the head prefect and he told us to do something and we didn't like it, and we held him by the ankles through an upstairs open window over the quadrangle, and we were seen doing this, and it didn't go down at all well. (*Brian Gray, schoolboy, 1940s*)

I can remember a classic ink fight when I was a child... during one lesson the ink wells had just been topped-up, and a guy put his pen in the inkpot and had too much ink on it, and without thinking he flicked the surplus off, and it went over the guy who was

sitting next to him, over his work. And this guy was well off, because he had a fountain pen, which was not very common... So he flicked the ink back on the other guy's page. So with that, the other kid took out the ink well and he poured it all over this kid's work. Well, this kid emptied his fountain pen... it squirted out the end, so he used it like an ink pistol, and he squirted his fountain pen at this chap straight in the face. And I'll never forget to this day, this guy got up and got the earthenware pot, full of ink, off of the window ledge, and he just tipped it over

Florence Porteous, about 1916.

'till a teacher came round the corner, and then we'd run out of the gate, so that the teacher would run down the road, because we'd get a bigger thrill out of it... I had no respect for Priory School when I was there, it was something that was foisted upon us... I just never felt as though it was my school. (*Graham Fletcher, schoolboy, 1970s*)

I didn't used to like school a lot, so I just used to go in one door, and go over the back wall, go down the beach or something... Next door to the school there was a picture house, which was the Odeon at the time. When I was in secondary school I used to fit through the toilet window, so I sort of skived school and if it was a miserable day... [of] course the toilet window was nearly always broken, so I just used to climb through there and sit in the picture house watching the films. (*Keith Ayres, schoolboy, 1970s*)

Youth clubs

Youth clubs have always been a popular venue for young people, often being the only place to meet members of the opposite sex; they also helped with the transition from child to young adult.

Yes there was smoking and girls in the cycle racks and behind the youth club... oh yes, you almost had to... The cycle sheds was the place to be, and they were big cycle sheds... very, very big cycle

this guy's head. Well, you can imagine the mess there was. I mean it was unbelievable! I mean, nobody knew quite what to do with him because every time they moved him it left a trail of ink. They sort of wrapped him up in newspaper and carted

him off down to the sluice, and it was quite amazing. (*David Reeves, schoolboy, 1950s*)

I used to play truant quite a lot, and it was so easy to play truant at this particular school... we used to stand by the gate, wait

sheds... And the other place was behind the youth club, we had a youth club at the school, which was in the school grounds but not exactly tied to the school itself... the best evening being

Paul Barratt (left) and friends, early 1970s.

Friday evenings, where you'd have live bands on. Manfred Mann made a start there... it was a very popular youth club... (*Paul Barratt, teenager, 1960s*)

Provided you went to the church and subsequently went to the Sunday School you could actually go to the youth club that the church ran, Saturday evening... Looking back on it, it was just an opportunity for the boys to meet the girls really, they had a sort of, it wasn't a coffee bar, it was a drinks bar, and you could buy sweets and things, and we played table tennis and volleyball, and there was a kind of disco running... and gradually as time went on, boy met girl and girl met boy, and your eyes met across the room and you started getting together, I got involved with this young lady, and we had our close encounters in the back of a Morris Minor on top of the hill... I must have been 17... still going to the youth club

because this was after the youth club that we usually went up... (*Neville Penter, teenager, 1960s*)

Before I left school we spent most of it [spare time] hanging around in friends' houses usually. I had a couple of really good friends who used to come round and sit in our dining room, they were never allowed to go upstairs, so we always used to sit in the dining room, or just hang about in the streets really. I think for a while we went to this derelict house just to hang out in there for some reason, there was nothing there, but it was somewhere to go. There was a youth club, called Point Seven, which I started going to, but I never told my Mum that that's where I went, because I knew that if I'd told her she wouldn't let me go, because she thought it was a rough area down at Point Seven... I suppose they played music and there were soft drinks. (*Gail Stewart-Bye, teenager, 1970s–'80s*)

Gail Stewart-Bye (centre) aged 16.

I go to [the] youth club every Thursday... near the Salisbury pub, Cosham... play pool, watch telly, talk, that's all really... socialise. (*Arran Stevens, teenager, 1990s*)

Throughout the century music and image were a fundamentally intrinsic part of being a teenager or young person. This often manifested itself in the form of 'cult' following.

In 1963 I was 16 and the Beatles certainly transformed my life as a teenager, the Beatles and the Rolling Stones, the Swinging Blue Jeans, the Searchers... and, in 1963, when they came on the market if you were 16 years old, it was a wonderful era. It just transformed your life, you know, what before had been a fairly mundane music scene was transformed by the Beatles and all these people. (*Ernest Aspey, teenager, 1960s*)

One such 'cult', which developed during the 1950s, was the Teddy Boys.

I'd see the teddy boys in their scarlet coats, long drape coats and funny trousers and hairdos, I remember very well, and also the skinheads of course; they were quite a part of Portsmouth and, of course, at that time Portsmouth was a flourishing naval base and there used to be trouble between the local lads and the navy guys. By the time I started going out, sort of socially, as a teenager or in middle teens, most of that sort of thing had

Hanging about on street corners is nothing new! Marie Spraggs outside her parents shop, 1940. The young man was a Free French sailor.

died out but apparently there were some pretty horrendous situations in some of the clubs and pubs around Portsmouth at that time, brawls, and what-have-yous... I felt they were colourful, but I also felt that they were a threat to me as a person I suppose. I could say, grandly, a threat to society. I suppose they were, in as much as they were knocking the traditional values, but I always felt that I would be very wary if I was out and met any of them... (*Dave Reeves*)

Some young men had no inclination to become a teddy boy themselves.

Basically if I had become a Ted in 1963, I wouldn't have been 'in', to quote a phrase of the time. I had a fairly neutral attitude to everything. I used to have a Beatle haircut and a combat jacket, which was the wartime combat jacket, but seemed to be the 'in' thing. Which led you to think that I was going through a sort of 'mod-ish' existence, but I tried not to be like the Mods who came in about the same year. The mods used to wear those big tank jackets and had scooters. I tried not to go in for that... I didn't have a Beatles' suit, some friends of mine had Beatles' suits made, or bought rather. Again this was all fashion. The Beatles wore Beatle suits at their early concerts and everyone wanted to wear one. (*Ernest Aspey, teenager, 1960s*)

You had the mods and the rockers... all sorts of things happened around about 1964, the

Beatles arrived, there was this shift in emphasis from a society run by older people to a society not run by younger people, but influenced very strongly by the younger generation. You had 'pirate' radio and society was definitely challenged in the '60s and it all seemed to happen together. (*Terry Chase, teenager, 1960s*)

The late 1970s brought new challenges to the social order; Gerard Bye recalled punk rockers.

We thought it was a complete change from glam rock. A refreshing change, actually. It was wild and exciting because it was so outrageous, the things they sang. They were very outspoken, rude, and we liked it because it was naughty of course... They weren't a threat, they were something new, creative, a new sound, it was wonderful. It was our sound, because it was created in our time. They were considered a threat, but that happened to the Beatles in their time. (*Gerard Bye, teenager, 1970s*)

In the post-war period many youngsters were influenced by American trends, in particular jukeboxes and coffee bars became a popular alternative to youth clubs, they were also seen as a more 'grown up' choice.

Because it was like Yankee land, which was what we used to call America in those days... the jukebox was like the closest most

of us got, other than the cinema, to the Yankee Land, which was like Disneyland, Dreamland, for us as kids growing up, you know, and so the coffee bars and that was like it gave you, it was like growing up... (*Mike Hancock, teenager, 1950s-'60s*)

What were they like?

They were great... There used to be one on the corner of Marmion Road and we used to go in and have a cup of coffee and then ride down to the fun fair and see if there were any young ladies around and then back to the coffee bar. Of course when you'd passed your test you could

Chris Spendlove on his Lambretta, about 1965.

Alice and William Perkins with their daughter Gwen, about 1920.

did feel slightly silly when the girls said, "are you going to buy us a coffee then?" (*Mike Hancock, teenager, late 1950s*)

The facts of life

Throughout the century both adults and children apparently found sex education a difficult subject to broach.

My mother didn't tell me anything, you just used your own common sense... it was a girls' school... you never spoke about it and even in the schools your teacher never said anything about that. (*Anonymous schoolgirl, 1920s–'30s*)

I remember going in there, and there was my brother born... and I said, "I wonder where he came from" and nobody said. I wanted to ask really, but of course, I wouldn't ask my mother... but I guessed. She looked just the same as normal... We just assumed that the woman was cut open and the baby taken out. There was no other way in which it could happen, was there! (*A child in the 1920s*)

I didn't know where my baby was coming from... I thought they were going to cut me open and the baby was going to come out where the navel is. (*Emma Smith, expectant mother, 1930s*)

We used to think if you kissed a boy you would get pregnant... It didn't occur to us anything else had to happen... We didn't know

actually take the girl on the back of the bike. And that was really great, that. (*David Reeves, teenager, 1950s–'60s*)

You'd hang around on the rail outside if you didn't have any money. If you had money you'd go inside... buying an ice cream, a coffee, or a coke and you'd sort of chat them [girls] up there. I can remember sort of feeling 'Jack the Lad'. Of course, 'Jack the Lad' was okay, but he didn't have any money and the one thing the girls wanted was someone who was going to buy 'em a drink or an ice cream... You

about that sort of thing. (*Anonymous teenager, 1930s*)

You certainly didn't have any [sex education] at school, and as I recall what I got at home was fairly limited. You were told what you absolutely had to know as late as possible, it wasn't volunteered very early, and it was all handled... really it was something you didn't want to talk about too much... (*Sue Spencer, teenager, 1950s*)

My parents found it very difficult... to talk to us about it, I was given a book, and I was told to go and read it and come back and ask any questions... It was terrible because it didn't actually

tell you anything... When I came to tell my kids... it was much more interactive, my kids have known about it from the age of two or three... My parents gave us this book, they said "Ask us any questions". I didn't know what questions to ask at that time... (*Neville Penter, child, 1960s*)

I was about eight or something, well they told you some stuff in school, but you get a load of stuff off the TV, and Mum did tell us some stuff as well... that's what most people talk about half of the time. Now I talk to my friends and stuff, it's easy... it's much easier talking to friends. (*Louise Egan, child, 1990s*)

Married life

For many people, particularly before World War Two, sex went hand-in-hand with marriage, in other words, it was not to be indulged in unless, or until, you were within the respectable confines of married life.

There's one price for a girl, and that's a wedding ring, and you don't sell yourself for anything less than that, or else you are no good. (*Anonymous interviewee recalling her mother's opinion about sex before marriage, 1930s*)

Lil [interviewee's sister], she had a white wedding... I was behind,

Bridesmaids at the wedding of Alderman Porter's younger daughter, Violet, in 1921, surrounded by a crowd of onlookers.

Sidney and Joy Hobbs on their wedding day during World War Two.

proud as a little peacock... I was about eight, something like that... There was our own family there, and his family, and a couple of the well-known neighbours, but of course it wasn't [a] big wedding [like] you have today. All Saints' Church. (*Anonymous child, 1920*)

My father wanted me to wait for a big wedding, I didn't want to... there wasn't the money about... We got married... and we went to Kimbell's, there was about 20 of us. That was lovely, and we had a spread and everything, and it was in March... then we went and had a walk, and it was bitterly cold... (*Emma Smith, bride, 1937*)

Joy Hobbs got married during the war so had more to worry about than the day

itself. Her friends and family went to great lengths to ensure a good day, despite shortages.

Well my father kindly gave me coupons he had been saving for a suit and I was able to go and buy a dress. My mother tried to get me into a white dress for a white wedding and she kept borrowing from various friends who had dresses but I never wanted to have a white dress... none of the frocks she borrowed fitted me so I was able to go and buy a frock, which was a pinky shade with brown accessories... Well you could still get a good fruit cake then. I had two tiers and the marzipan was put through the middle of the cake instead of on top, and you had cardboard covers that were decorated with Plaster of Paris flowers and things, so it looked as if it was a white cake... (*Joy Hobbs, bride, 1940s*)

It seems some people were so overwhelmed by the day they couldn't actually remember it too well!

... Fareham Registry Office, autumn wedding, beautiful weather, Carol was in lemon. [Was it a long dress?] Oh yeah, yeah, long, no, was it a long dress? You've got me thinking on that one now, not overly long, no, no. Well attended, I think we had something like 70 people at the wedding, in the reception. Yes it was a day I'll certainly remember. (*Paul Barratt, bridegroom, 1986*)

... a fairly traditional style wedding... I wore an ivory dress, an embroidered ivory dress, with a short veil, and I had fresh flowers in my hair, and a fresh bouquet... I had four bridesmaids... and they were all in lemon... little sort of ballerina style dresses... and the men wore morning suits... We got married at John Pounds in Old Portsmouth, partly because it was our parish, and partly because my husband had been married before... [it was one of the few churches in Portsmouth which would marry divorcees] (*Gail Stewart-Bye, bride, 1989*)

Childbirth

The 1990s experience of childbirth was often considerably different to that of the 1940s.

I went into hospital. We had to pay then to go in, it wasn't free. I can't remember how much we paid, I know I went in there for a day and a night and I came out the next day, in the July, because I had false labour. And they charged me for that bit of time I was in there. And then of course they kept you in for 10 days. I can't remember how much we paid, but I know I used to pay back 6d a week to the hospital till it was paid... (*Mrs Chase, young mother pre-NHS, 1940s*)

I went in on Sunday and was out again the next day, I only stayed overnight. (*Nicole Pitman, mother, 1990s*)

Nicole and Hannah Pitman.

Illness associated with pregnancy was common and sometimes led to tragedy.

... I thought to myself, well she's going to have better care going in hospital than have it at home... I booked her into a nursing home... and I paid a deposit, I always remember it, £10 deposit. She used to go there monthly... for a check up... before you could look round she was in hospital... in the water was albumin, they call it, which poisoned the water and they said that if the child is born... you won't have a wife and you won't have a child... as far as we're concerned the mother is the one; forget the child. So they'd fight for my wife's life... She was ill and they had to take the baby away from her... I cried my eyes out afterwards... (*Anonymous father, 1930s*)

Childhood illnesses, sickness and death

There were many common illnesses and diseases prevalent during the earlier half of the century, which although embarrassing for families at the time, were often seen as par for the course.

We used to have a few drops of Licel which was a very strong disinfectant and it was dripped in the bowl, just in drops, when our hair was rinsed, and we had to hide our forehead with a towel so that the water did not run down over our forehead and go into our eyes... she [interviewee's sister] had a disease they called ringworm and it was contagious and of course Mum assured herself that she must have picked it up at school and we were always told never to try on anybody's hat or use their comb... (*Vera Cole, child, 1910s*)

For some children only genuine illness resulted in special treatment at home, as one interviewee recalled when asked if she had a fire in her bedroom.

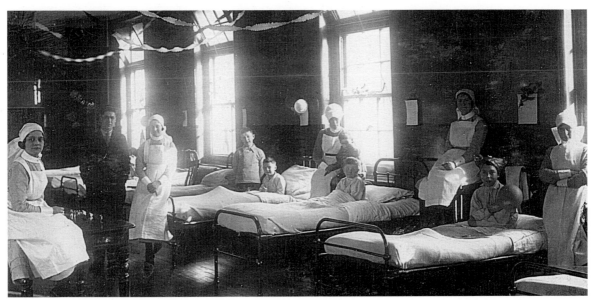

A children's ward in the Royal Portsmouth Hospital, 1931.

Mrs Florence Chiverton's first husband died leaving her with two young children. She is pictured here, in 1917, with her second husband, Charles Gaul, and daughters Ruby, Vera and Florence.

Only if we were ill. If we were ill, we might have a fire in the bedroom, but, then, my mother didn't allow us to be ill very often. We couldn't be ill very often. We mustn't be ill. She didn't recognise that. She would say "Get downstairs". She wasn't one to make sissies of us, but if you were ill, yes you would have a fire in the bedroom. (*Anonymous, child, 1920s*)

As a child it was very difficult to be ill in hospital, particularly before the war, as visiting hours were restricted. Doris Bealing remembered being a patient as a child in the Infectious Diseases Hospital at Milton.

... in those days your parents didn't come in. They didn't even come into the ward because we were infectious. We had to look through the glass door and they always used to leave a present for us and after they had gone the nurses would come round with trolleys and we would wait for these presents. I remember once they pushed a penny under the door to me. For a lot of time I was in a big ward with lots of children and we used to... push trolleys across from bed to bed at night... Part of the time I was in a room on my own, I think when I had the diphtheria... (*Doris Bealing, child, 1930s*)

It was equally difficult when a parent became ill:

My mother made herself very ill... she caught this germ... It is a disease... she got it all over her face... and their mind wanders... she used to say when she was in bed she could see little people on her pillow... one of us had to stay home from school to let the doctor in. (*Vera Cole, child, 1910s*)

Well, I think she had TB, and they kept taking her in hospital. They would build her up, and she would come out all nice, and we thought everything was all right, and then, of course, she would go right back again because she was giving us what she should have had herself really, but we didn't know that. (*Anonymous, talking about her mother's fatal illness, 1920s*)

I think they used to pay twopence a week to belong to a doctor... over in Arundel Street... there used to be a doctor's surgery over there that if you had bad colds or anything, because I went for my Dad, and you paid a shilling a bottle, and it was good, they used to make up the bronchial mixture... when I had my [daughter] when she was ill, you had to pay for the doctor then, and that was half a crown a time, if they came, and it was a lot. (*Emma Smith, early 1930s, before the advent of the NHS*)

Early death was far more common than now.

My oldest sister died, she had blood poisoning, she had a foot blister that went septic, and they said she had the early stages of scarlet fever, which I then caught and I was in hospital for 13 weeks. I then had what they called nasal diphtheria as well. (*Doris Bealing, child, 1930s*)

Funerals

Until the late 1960s, preparation of the body was usually done by a member of the family or a friend, often an older woman. It was also traditional for the body to be laid out at home. Only in the latter part of the century were undertakers used for the whole process.

A 1920s funeral, with the coffin, unusually, carried on a steam lorry.

Alan Masters, sadly killed in a road accident in 1952 when aged seven.

My father died about 11 o'clock in the evening, and we couldn't contact my youngest brother until the next morning... we had to go round to the doctor's to get the death certificate... In the meantime, my brother... came round to the house on his own... and he'd washed my Dad. He'd found him in the front room... I went in just to see him just before they screwed him down... He was downstairs. I wasn't exactly frightened, but it's not something you enjoyed... and the smell as you walked in was quite overpowering, whatever they used... In those days, everybody had their dead in their house... It was a burial. It was nothing exceptional. It was the Co-op. We always had the Co-op... Dad was buried up at Milton Cemetery. It's never a nice day when you go to a funeral. (*Ruth Williams, teenager, 1940s*)

I can remember one or two of my older great aunties dying, but as children we were kept pretty much away from it [funerals]... it was not until I was up in my late teens that I actually went to a funeral and it did tend to be very much a male-dominated situation, the women would tend to look after all the people who were coming to the house... if the coffin was at the house then they would look after the people... they would prepare all the food for the funeral wake, but actually going to the funeral for the most part tended to be the men of the family... One of my aunties, in particular, was a person who was called on by a lot of friends and neighbours... to lay out the body so it was ready for the funeral people to come and collect the body, but I think by then we were just about getting to the stage where more people were being dealt with by the undertakers. (*Sue Spencer, young mother, 1960s*)

My Dad's – we didn't go to the actual funeral. I think just the eldest two went... My Dad's funeral was very, very big... I think nuns did the laying out, it was a very big funeral. I mean my Dad's brother was a priest, so he was one of the priests at the funeral and he was quite good friends with the canon. The local bishop did the main Mass, there was five priests there, there were photographs and it made the local papers and so on, you know, sort of very big funeral with lots of cars and people coming over from Ireland and so on. There were telegrams from politicians in Ireland and stuff... his family were quite well known. (*Anonymous, 1970s*)

EARNING A CRUST

John Stedman, Katy Ball and Sharon Lee

WORK is central to most people's lives. It occupies a large part of their time, it helps define their place in the world, and its rewards determine their standard of living. Portsmouth people have shared with their fellow Britons many changes in working practices. The greatest has been in the increased number of married women working outside the home. The working week is generally much shorter now than in 1900, when most people worked nine hours a day, five and a half days a week. Long apprenticeships have been replaced by shorter training, some of it provided by bodies such as Highbury College.

There have been marked changes in the pattern of local trades. Portsmouth had many naval tailors in 1900, while one company, Gieves, had already spread nationally. The shrinking size of the navy has almost wiped out the trade in Portsmouth. The lingerie trade employed thousands of people until the 1970s. Aircraft manufacture came in 1933 with Airspeed, and went in 1968. Other significant new employers have been linked to new technologies: Marconi (now Astrum) and IBM, which brought its UK headquarters here in 1971.

George Curtis and his wife Maria met in Greece during the war. He is working at his knife-grinding machine in Southsea, 1948.

Small local firms have been displaced or swallowed up by national chains. Pinks', a Portsmouth grocery chain flourishing in 1900, has disappeared, as have the bakeries Vospers and Campions (bought out by Spillers in the early 1960s). Timothy White's, which sold chemist's and home ware goods, itself became a regional chain before World War Two, but lost its identity after merger with Boots. By 1959 Brickwoods was the sole survivor, after merger and takeovers, of the 11 breweries Portsmouth had in 1900. Brickwoods became part of Whitbreads in 1971 and its brewery in Queen Street ceased production in 1983. The city's

largest employers now are the National Health Service and the council. The range of tasks undertaken by local government is enormous, ranging from maintaining roads to organising the city arts festival.

Getting a job

Before 1945 getting a job was not easy and the position of employees was weak. Knowing someone in the organisation concerned was often important.

I definitely wanted to get on the corporation [passenger transport dept] and I tried and tried. Ben

Louis Bushill, photographed in 1974 when a bus inspector.

(Louis Bushill, employed by the City of Portsmouth Passenger Transport Dept, 1934–76)

... the Chief Constable of Portsmouth used to go to this farm on holidays. I was talking to him one day; he was Welsh, obviously, and he asked me what I was going to do, and I told him I had no idea, and he suggested I come to Portsmouth and join the Portsmouth Police Fire Brigade as, what was known then, as a Boy Fireman. Well, that sounded quite useful to me. My mother and father were not keen on the idea, but I had my own way and came down to Portsmouth round about the beginning of 1937. *(Goronwy Evans, born in Monmouthshire)*

To get a skilled job normally involved serving an apprenticeship of five years. Before World War Two the child's parents paid a fee or 'consideration'.

I was an indentured apprentice [to a court costumier in Southsea]. 5s a week and then, after six months, I had 7s. 6d. a week. What can you do with that with a girl who's growing and working in a high-class shop and needs to dress appropriately?... I believe they paid £10 for my indentures, which was about ten weeks of dad's wages. *(Eileen Rayner, apprenticed 1919)*

My brother, who was six years older than me, was only earning a nominal wage. He worked for a firm called Winterbottoms in Stamshaw, a printing firm.

Hall was the general manager at the time, and he got fed up with me in the end and he ordered me out of the office. And he said, "Look, all things being equal, when your time comes up you're on the list, when your time comes up you'll be on it". A job for life with a pension was the ultimate. In Depression days I'm talking about, before the war. So, anyway, as I came out of the office I met a lady who I use to go to school with her son... She said, "What are you doing, Lou?" I told her, and she said, "Leave it to me". This is the honest truth. In less than a fortnight, all things being equal, I was on the job! It's just who you know, ain't it?

Robert Hostler making rock, about 1965.

Because my father couldn't afford to pay his indentures for his apprenticeship, he was taken on on a very small wage. (*Jack Price, talking about 1931*)

In those days the local traders who wanted to employ a boy would come to the school and ask the masters if there was anybody there they could recommend for the job. Mr Corbin came to the school. He had a greengrocer's in Albert Road and he wanted a greengrocer's errand boy... After I had worked at the shop for a while, my cousin told me that the Post Office were recruiting for boy messengers and my mother said would I like to go and try for it. So I went and had an interview. Now in those days the Post Office used to have a policy of employing their own people's sons and second, orphan children. So I became a boy messenger. That was about when I was 14 and 3 months.... when I became 16 they introduced motor cycles and I became a motor cycle messenger for the next two years. (*Jack Price, left school about 1933*)

Some, however, had little choice of career. One boy's father started work in the family wheelwright's business, Hoad's, before he had even left school.

He was a young wheelwright. I remember he used to say to me that he had a clip round the ear because, although he was only about ten years old in those days, he'd turned up a wrong thread on a bolt – they were making some, I suppose, screws and bolts, you see, on the lathe, and he made a mistake, and his father gave him a clip round the ear... (*Bernard Hoad*)

Until shortly before World War Two dustmen were employed by the council only on a casual basis:

At Anglesea Road, Anglesea Yard, they had to stand outside the gate while the superintendent of cleansing picked out, physically, enough people to man the horse and carts and the other refuse vehicles, to pick the refuse up on a daily basis. So you can understand, you know, the old adage says "kissing goes by favour". If you were someone who was popular with the superintendent, you got the job. If you were someone who offended him you didn't get a job. (*Frank Deacon, cleansing dept employee and trade unionist*)

By the 1950s finding a job had become much easier as Britain had full employment and was even short of labour.

Oh, it was easy for me, so much so that every six months, when I was bored – although we didn't use that word then – when I thought I had learned everything in the job, I would move on, nearly doubling my money each time, until going into the WRNS. (*Diana Hart-Thomas, teenager in the 1950s*)

And we had a very difficult time during the 1950s, because we'd reach the stage of almost full employment, and... the pay was not particularly good,... we had a degree of problem in recruiting

people to work for us. And whilst we had a core of loyal people who had been with us forever and a day, whose books were kept well and who were cheerful and helpful and all the rest of it, there were others that came and went that were near criminals in my view! But you had to take what you could get. (*David Miles, Company Secretary, Campions the bakers*)

Learning the job

Some jobs provided formal training. Learning others was much more ad hoc.

I went and did my midwifery training... at the Royal Naval – Royal Marine Maternity Home... The Matron was Miss Richards and there was a sister in charge, and they both had very high standards. Miss Richards gave us our lectures, which were very good, and ran the home, and the sister was in charge of the practical side of it... The idea was to look after these naval wives and, not only deliver them safely of babies but also give them a rest and build them up, and I'm sure they enjoyed themselves... [After delivery a woman normally stayed for] Fourteen days, and she would be in bed for most of that time, which was rather a long time as opposed to now. (*Gladys Sweetnam – trained as a midwife in Portsmouth just before World War Two*).

We had a wonderful apprenticeship training scheme. We kept it up right to the end, actually [the company closed in 1983]. We kept to this 'one apprentice to three journeymen',

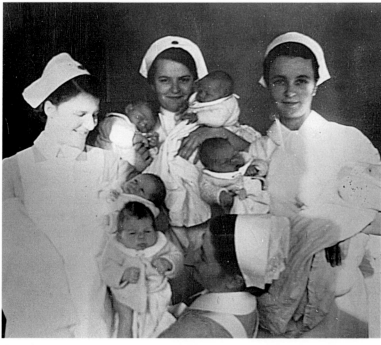

Gladys Sweetnam, colleagues and some of their charges, 1938.

White and Newton made furniture in Dunbar Road from 1924 until 1984.

and they did really work alongside the journeymen, so they had, sort of, first-hand teaching. And then, of course, backed up by the college [Highbury]. (*Paul Dryden, production manager of White & Newton, furniture makers*)

New employees were often subject to teasing, or even bullying.

One of the things I was warned on was to get my hair cut, get my hair combed and if I didn't they would glue my hair down. So being a cheeky kid and that, not worrying about it, I didn't bother, so they collared me one day and got me on the bench and glued my hair down... and carted

me downstairs – this was when the shop foreman was out of course, and they threw me in the pile of shavings behind the spindle machine, so I looked like a chicken, you know, all fluffed out like! (*Ken Freemantle, apprenticed as a carpenter, 1939*)

A new recruit would obviously be given some on-the-spot training by going out with another roundsman to see how he handled his cash, and how he determined his order for the ensuing day, and how he related the two and came in at the end of the day and paid in his cash... (*David Miles, Company Secretary, Campions the baker's, 1955–c.1965*)

In corset factories in the 1950s new girls started as runners, fetching for established workers and receiving wages.

You done running for six months and, in the meantime, you had to learn how to do seams and how to put garments together, how to put zips in, hooks and eyes and steels. Because we had corsets with steels down the front and we had to learn all that within six months and then you went on piecework, earned your own money. (*Helen Guest, runner and seamer, 1955–62*)

Well you had a lady who was the... she worked as an ordinary machinist, but she would teach you. You know, she was chosen to teach you.... But they were the girls who were already on the section. I think they maybe got a little bit more money for actually teaching us. (*Jackie Wilson, machinist, c.1955–60*)

Working conditions

Over the course of the century working conditions gradually improved and the general working environment relaxed. Relationships between staff and employers, and worker and public also changed, becoming more informal and less deferential. Danger was, and remains, ever-present in some occupations. Michael Turton was the third generation of his family to work on the

railway. His grandfather was 'a goods shunter in the yard'.

He had his legs chopped off in a railway accident in Fratton yard, both of them. Engine went over them. He slipped doing some shunting, and the engine went over his legs.... obviously he couldn't do shunting with wooden legs, so he was put on the platform at Fratton. (*Michael Turton, signalman 1953–1995*)

Building workers had one of the most dangerous occupations and, although standards have improved, it still has the highest death rate.

Len Kidd was one of the stonemasons who worked on the tower of the burnt-out Guildhall after World War Two, while Fred Grist was

one of a team repairing the harbour station.

Dangerous, too. We did manage to get thruppence an hour danger money then. There was a sheer drop, 173 feet, right into the basement. (*Len Kidd*)

If you wanted to go up a girder to fix a piece of steel you had to shin up the stanchions. There is an art in that boy, getting your feet on the outside and your knees on the inside and after a while it is quite easy to learn to shin up, you know 15 – 20 foot in the air without a ladder and then walk along the girders when you got up to the top... The only other way was riding the crane. They put a piece of steel on the crane, one chap would sit one end and another the other and ride up on the

Shunters, probably including Michael Turton's grandfather, about 1915.

crane, which is against the law really but it was an easy way of getting up. (*Fred Grist*)

Pay and perquisites gradually improved. In the Depression years of the 1930s job security and a pension were major issues.

Mainly the security of it, actually... if you can visualise what was happening at that time, jobs were few and far between, especially jobs that had a future, or some security, and I can always remember my father saying to me, "Oh yes, if you go into the police force, it's a pensionable job". (*Ken Hampton, fireman and police officer, joined 1935*)

Fresh cottage loaves at William Miller's bakery (later Campion's), about 1920.

... at one time in the building trade, the building industry – if you took holidays – you weren't paid, there was no holiday pay – as it is known now. If it rained and you were rained off, you weren't paid. If you were sick, you weren't paid. You supplied all your own tools and then the union, after a lot of effort, managed to get what was called a tool allowance. Which was 2d a day. It doesn't sound much but it was 1s a week tool money, which was supposed to replace the expendable tools. Like saw files. (*Ken Freemantle, carpenter, 1939–1989*)

In those days everyone was paid weekly. You got your little pay envelope with your pay slip in it every week. Massive sums of money! Mine was £6 10s. The girls used to have it all in the

envelopes ready with the names on, and then, department, by department, they would just go through and pass out the wages to each person. (*David Chamberlain, assistant buyer in a corset factory, 1956–57*)

Many businesses, like Campions, one of Portsmouth's bigger bakeries, introduced paid holiday in the 1930s.

I think there was a feeling that we, we the employees, were part of a family. This was enhanced, obviously, by a certain amount of altruism on the part of the directorate, so that the company was progressive in that my father enjoyed seven days holiday a year, but this was increased to ten days. That was paid holiday. My father would be required to

work on a Saturday, but he had a half-day, so his half-day was on a Wednesday. (*David Miles*)

Working hours have decreased.

When I worked at Weston Hart I used to work five-and-a-half days a week. I had Wednesday afternoon off... All your mates were working... and I was stuck on a Wednesday afternoon in Portsmouth... so I used to miss my mates and going off to football... and all your friends in the summer – they were off and I would be stuck behind the counter in the service department at 5 o'clock on a Saturday afternoon and it was terrible. So when I went to Portsmouth dockyard I had a five-day week automatically and, I think, about three times the wage. (*Ernest*

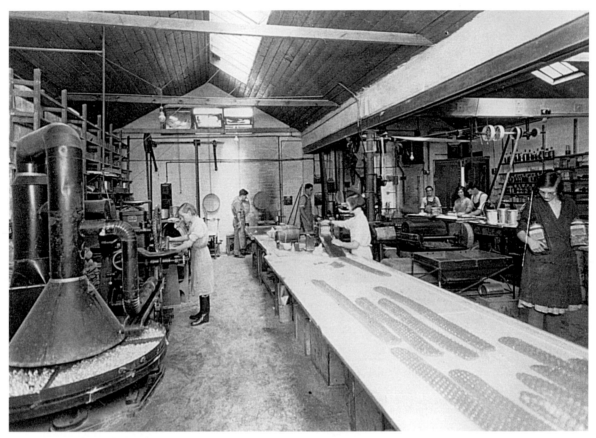

The Hostler sweet factory, Cosham Street, about 1930.

Aspey's first job was for a television engineers in Fratton Road. He moved on in 1965).

Dress codes have existed in most occupations.

But every morning old Newton had a ritual, before the shop was opened at nine o'clock, he always inspected the staff. Always walked round the back of them, looked at them, they held their hands out and he looked at their hands, and that was before the shop was open. (*Frank Deacon, worked in a pawnbroker's shop in the mid-1930s*)

I used to have to wear rather a biggish apron in the morning and a cap, but in the afternoon she used to like me to change into a neat, clean frock, usually a brown or a blue one, with a little tiny pinafore and a cap and little white cuffs in case visitors came.

Repairing a bus engine, Highland Road depot, 1970s.

So I used to have to change into that. But she provided those for me. I didn't have to buy those. (*Mabel Pearce, domestic servant in the late 1930s*)

When we went on the vegetable round that was a different matter, you were dressed in a collar and tie, the three days a week we went on the vegetable round you was dressed up properly. (*Harry Cullimore, greengrocer and coal merchant from World War One until the 1960s.*)

As late as 1971 female council workers were obliged to wear skirts.

I wore trousers and was taken into my senior officer's office and told it couldn't be done. No matter how cold it was, I was the supervisor and I should be setting an example. Certainly they couldn't have ladies in trousers. (*Diana Hart-Thomas*)

IBM definitely had a culture. We wore suits and white shirts – that was expected even if you were just working in an ordinary job and never meeting a customer. That's changed over recent years, as I said, the whole culture and outlook of business as a whole has changed and people are much more relaxed... Most people in the company these days [1998] do not wear a suit unless they are customer-facing or going out to see a customer. (*Phil Wrixton, employee of IBM since the 1970s*)

The amount of physical labour and discomfort in many occupations has been reduced by technological change. In 1953 signal boxes were full of levers that operated points by pulling rods connected by cranks, and semaphore signals by pulling wires, but they were modernised by the 1980s and the Portsmouth area was, thereafter, controlled by a single box at Jacob's Ladder.

It was said at that time that it was the most demanding job, and they were the fittest men in the country, because every muscle in your body was used... The old mechanical signalmen lived a

Portcreek Junction signal box, 1968. Signalmen had no breaks but snatched meals between trains.

longer life than what the modern signalman lives... Well, it was all worked by track circuits and buttons and little switches, mainly. The mechanical pulling of levers had all gone: the points were worked by motors, the signals were all coloured lights and certain sections, like between Portscreek and Fratton, was automatic, so was between the high level and the harbour worked by track circuit... you become a button pusher, you've got no exercise... (*Michael Turton, signalman 1953–95*)

They [tramdrivers] didn't have a very good job weather wise, stuck out in the weather, cold, freezing. I've seen them come in the car sheds with ice in their eyebrows. Well, you know, it was foggy and that turned to ice, but they used to dress up well, sort of mackintosh aprons. (*Charles Eames, conductor on the Portsdown & Horndean Light Railway, 1921–35*)

Some of Portsmouth's citizens face other potential problems.

Sometimes from clients, not direct racism... Most of my colleagues are from banking backgrounds so I wouldn't say they are racist or anything, just some of them never met people from a different culture. Different. No, I have never met racism within my organisation I can't say I have. (*Rumal Khan, business advisor*)

Almost every workplace generated social activity – sports teams, dinners.

I can't speak high enough for the corporation because they had everything, not only for your working life, for your private life as well. You had a darts team, a billiards team, a football team, a band and a club, which was included for parties for children... (*Louis Bushill, employed by the City of Portsmouth Passenger Transport Dept, 1934–76*)

But some occupations have hardly changed at all, for example, working in catering, which is intensely pressured at times and often involves anti-social hours.

Great fun... sometimes I was reduced to tears on a Sunday afternoon when it was so busy and all the customers would be shouting for service and we didn't know where to turn. (*Lydia Briano, member of the family and waitress at Verrecchia's*)

I like working in Portsmouth College very much. My colleagues, my line manager, they're very nice people and I do enjoy it very much, although restaurant work was different, mostly night, college work during the daytime. What I see now – I can spend more time with my family. In the restaurant, when I was working in the restaurant, I didn't have much time in my hand to spend with my family, in the college, here, I can do that. I can have better family life, than when I work in a restaurant, yeah. (*Ebandur Chowdhury*)

The café on Clarence Esplanade in the 1920s.

Portsmouth trades

Besides the dockyard, two industries were particularly important in Portsmouth during the century: the corset industry and aircraft manufacture. There were few jobs for women in Portsmouth beside shop work and domestic service, so their wages were low and that had attracted corset manufacturers in the 19th century. In 1901 there were 15 corset factories in Portsmouth, employing 2,288 people, mostly women. Now there are two.

You were there before half past seven, the steam came on at half past seven. And you just sat down and you worked. We could talk to each other across the benches, so that you often said what you did the night before, you know like, and what boyfriend you went out with that night. And you often went to dancing. But we talked. But then our main thing was to earn the money, you see. Your forewoman, they called them in those days, she sat at the end of the room on a long table. And when you'd finished... you had... the work was packed in 12s... And then the forewoman gave you another lot to come back and do... And you worked steadily till lunchtime. And then after that you worked till half-past-five. But you didn't leave your machine until the buzzer went!... We had huge wheels underneath the benches that had a strap to come up and work your machine, you had a

treadle. But you got used to it. I had lots of needles in my fingers, but still never mind. You go, "anyone with a pair of pliers please?" (*Florrie Allnutt, machinist and supervisor at Leethems [Twilfits], 1928–73*)

First it came to us in a bundle of all cut out, 12, like, panels. We would seam the panels together, then they would go on to a department called the binders, flat binders. They opened the seams and flat binded all the seams opened down. Then they would come back to us again and we would put in a zip or whatever it had to have, if steels it would have steels. That would go back to the anglers, they would angle on, which is a zigzag. You would know it as a zigzag, but we called them anglers. They would go around the bottom, angling, putting on the suspenders for the stockings and then they would come back to us to the bones, put the bones on. You had bones about ten inches long down the sides and at the back. Really painful. But the delicate ones, you know, like the 1603s, they would go to the overlockers. We would put all the darts together in the front – the inside and the outside darts. There were six on each side and they all had to match – the darts – as they came together. We used to number them to make sure they matched. They go to the overlockers. They would overlock all the fronts of the darts and they would come back to us to turn under then it would go to the fancy stitch department that feather stitched, put them

together to make sure that the darts – if there was a dart out of place, we had an inspectress up the hatch – Betty Johnson – and she would hold the garments up, measure that all the bones matched together, all the darts matched, there was nothing poking out of the zips or anything, or she would have it back to repair as a reject. But that was it. (*Helen Guest, seamer at Weingarten's, 1955–62*)

You could wear whatever you liked. Most of us wore an apron, because we could keep our scissors in there or our bits and pieces. One of these little half aprons. But you could wear whatever you liked. And again I mentioned in there, if you were going to a do in the evening, you would pin your hair up in the morning, and go to work with a scarf on. (*Jackie Wilson, machinist, c.1955–60*)

I went back as an overlooker... But it was, like, examine all the corsets before they left for the end of that, you know, make sure everything was right. There was lots wrong, very often, sometimes out of six dozen you'd get a dozen things that wanted put right... you had to take them back to the machinist for them to put it right, you know. (*Edith Goodyear, worked at Chilcot & Williams, 1923–40*)

When we had no work we all used to bring our knitting in, it was ever so good! I mean they wouldn't allow it nowadays, but we used to sit there for hours until some work came up and

Helen Guest and friends at Weingarten's corset factory, late 1950s.

then the forelady used to give it out to who was waiting longest sort of thing. But we never ever got sent home. (*Doreen Kemp, flat binder, 1945–99*)

Men worked in the factories maintaining the sewing machines, printing boxes, cutting the fabric, in the warehouses and in the offices. Most of the managers were men.

Well, when I came out of the RAF, I went into hospital and had a lung removed and I had to get a job. So, I just looked at the papers and there was a job going. It was for an assistant buyer, and the specialist at the hospital had

said to me, "You want a light, indoor job", so I thought, well I'll go and see if I can get it. The Assistant Buyer was the title. The job was actually working in the warehouse, but on a salary, so that they could get me in on a Saturday and often on a Sunday without paying me any overtime. (*David Chamberlain, assistant buyer, Weingarten's, 1956–57*)

The design of Portsmouth-made corsets has followed fashion throughout the century and the decline of corset wearing in the 1960s nearly killed the trade. Modern corsets are not primarily about giving the wearer an 'ideal' body shape.

You had the 1905s [the number of a design], that was a girdle, just a girdle with 4 suspenders on, a waist girdle. Then you had the full ones – corselette they were called – corselettes. Then you had the... old-fashion ones with the steels, the bones all the way around, we had those. We had the 1603 which was like a panty girdle and they were all darts down the front, all silk, you know, pink silk nylon. There were quite a few other designs but all near enough the same around then. (*Helen Guest, seamer at Weingarten's, 1955–62*)

Well, just the basic one you wear as an outerwear thing, just like a push-up corset, and then they've

A cutter at Leethems, 1970.

got the more fancy ones with the lace and the suspenders and leather. We do leather, PVC, satin, denim – quite a variety really. They're basically the same, it's just they get, like, a little bit longer, or you get a full cup instead of half a cup, or something like that. (*Brenda Hulme, machinist, c.1965–2002*)

The factories were almost always remembered with affection.

It was lovely, best friends you ever had, they really were lovely girls. Everyone knew everybody. Always having a laugh and a joke and our coach trips were fabulous, really fabulous. I don't remember any rows or anything there, like they do today. And if you wanted – if anyone wanted any help – you went and helped them. (*Helen Guest, seamer at Weingarten's, 1955–62*)

Airspeed came to Portsmouth from York in 1933, the year after the city opened its airport. The company then had about 50 employees. It grew to nearly 1,000 employees by 1939. Most of the pre-war aircraft were wooden-framed. The company's designs were innovative, and included the

first commercial aircraft with a retractable undercarriage.

I started work as I left school, as apprentice carpenter and joiner... and prior to Airspeed I was working at a furniture factory on the industrial site at Wembley Stadium... I heard about the job through the local paper... I applied for the job, had a reply from them, and they then asked me if I would accept a position there as an aircraft woodworker... (*L. Munden, joined Airspeed in 1936*)

I was also involved with a certain amount of work with Couriers. Now Couriers were the original aircraft with a retractable undercarriage, single-engine, and they were used around Portsmouth. People remember seeing them as the ferry between Portsmouth and the Isle of Wight, run by the Portsmouth and Isle of Wight Aviation Co. With the Envoy, one thing I was involved with was a conversion of a standard Envoy for the King's Flight... (*V.G. Owen*)

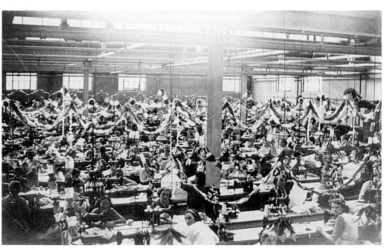

Leethems' (Twilfits) corset factory at Christmas in the 1930s.

Airspeed workers with the spars of a wing, mid-1930s.

Wages, in those days, as I say, eventually I was on a wage which was considered a very good wage in them days, I think it was about £3 12s [£3.60] a week. (*Mr Palmer, Airspeed worker who came from York*)

I played for several years with Airspeed football team in those days... Bill Bailey was the goalkeeper. We were in the Portsmouth league... we played on the aerodrome, we had a football pitch on the aerodrome. (*L. Munden*)

Airspeed was undercapitalised and, before the war, lurched from crisis to crisis. The company was saved by **the Oxford, a twin-engined aircraft adopted by the RAF for training bomber crews. Neville Shute Norway was Airspeed's first Managing** **Director, ousted in a boardroom coup in 1938. He afterwards became famous as novelist, writing under his first two names.**

A party given for children of Airspeed employees, c.1938. (By courtesy of *The News*)

The Airspeed factory, 1933 or 1934.

Norway comes into my office on a Friday morning and says, "Tiltman, what are we going to do? We've got the wages to pay this evening and we haven't got a bean in the world!"... I was petrified because I knew things were bad, but I didn't know it was as bad as that. So Norway says, "Well, there's only one thing to do – we'll get the chap who goes and fetches the wages usually, we get him up into this office and we'll brief him very carefully. We'll say to him 'You've got to go into the bank whistling as if you hadn't got a care in the world and then you've just got to slap it on the bench and say 'Wages, please!'." Nobody could think of a better way of doing it so we briefed him just like that. And he did this and he got away with it! (*Hessell Tiltman, Airspeed's chief designer*)

Now the Oxford was really a development of the Envoy... That order came through from the Ministry of Aircraft Production, I think some time in 1938, at a time when the firm was in a crisis and there was some worry, I did not doubt, that it would survive. The machine, the Oxford, was ordered straight off the drawing board. (*V.G. Owen*)

In 1940 a larger rival, de Havillands, acquired a majority of Airspeed shares. After the war, Airspeed made an airliner, the Ambassador and, later, parts for de Havilland aircraft, such as the Sea Vixen fighter and the Comet airliner. De Havilland formally took over the company in 1951. The factory finally closed altogether in 1968 when production of the Trident airliner was switched to the north.

I think it was all political, a lot of it, 'cause it wasn't two or three months before they closed it Statham [works manager] told us "We've got work for years"... they got a contract to build about 30 extended Tridents and he said, "We've got enough work to last years". (*Reg Milne, Airspeed worker, 1950s & '60s*)

Miscellaneous trades

Besides the occupations that are particularly identified with Portsmouth, as in all cities there were many others. Perhaps the most common of these before World War Two was domestic service.

I went into service – at a Lieutenant-Commander's house in Laburnum Grove – worked for him and his wife who was a cripple, and used to do everything in the house apart from the actual cooking. The lady herself supervised that, but I used to do everything else, washing and ironing, everything appertaining to the household, helping her, even, to get dressed and wash, because she couldn't do everything for herself. And I used to get 10s a week for that and all my food... I'd get up, make a pot of tea for both of them... take it up to them, and then I would have to wash the front down, do the brasses, do the passage right through, light the fire in the winter, and then lay the breakfast. Mr Ferris would get the breakfast. I used to have breakfast with him because Madam used to have hers upstairs. And then after that it was whatever rooms she desired, bedrooms or the downstairs, whichever Madam told me to do I had to do. And in my evenings, if she wanted me to do the silver out of the cabinets, I did the silver or the brass. Either that, or it was ironing, but she also liked to play games – board games – and her husband wasn't very keen, so invariably I used to get roped in for doing that as well, which was – it was very nice... I used to get up at about half-six and it'd be a quick wash and quickly get on with everything for the day, because the quicker I got finished doing it I could then get a little time to myself in the sitting room in the evening before Madam wanted other things done... I used to hope to be finished by about half-four or five o'clock and then get changed to do the tea. And then after that,

Building work, such as that on the site of the former Victoria Barracks in 1969, was transformed by the introduction of power tools and diggers.

hopefully... I could have a couple of hours to myself. And I used to have an afternoon off a week there. That was usually on a Wednesday afternoon. Directly after I'd finished scrubbing up the kitchen floor after washing up the dinner things I could go... but I had to be in by half-past nine. Mr Ferris didn't like you coming in late, so half-past nine it had to be. Very often I missed the last of the picture if I'd gone to the pictures because I had to be back in the house. *(Mabel Pearce, in service in the mid-1930s)*

Well, I just took the children out, bathed them and seen to their clothes and done things like that. As the years went on, and they grew up, I started doing the housework. You know, waiting on the table and that. It was only just like a couple with the three

children, but they were Jewish people and every Friday night it used to be a big do, you know, they had the fish and that... Of course, I was helping with everything then. In the beginning, they used to have a lady come in to do the scrubbing or whatever it was. That's how I gone on, like that, until I got married. *(Anonymous, in service from age 14, in 1931)*

Portsmouth had a small fishing fleet.

I used to go with my father onto Bath Square and the bar was opened at four o'clock in the morning – and as they were waiting for the ship to come in they used to go and have a drink before they off-loaded, and they used to off-load stuff there at Point... They used to lay the boxes out and it was sold – they auctioned it. (*Son of a fish salesman, born 1908*)

Hoad's was established as a wheelwrights and coachbuilders before 1900 and began making motorcars. In 1906 some petrol caught fire and the premises at Kingston Cross were burnt out. The business was re-established in Basin Street.

It was my grandfather's brother Herbert, and his two sons, Jeff and Bert, who ran the business of wheelwrights... the actual premises were relatively dilapidated; they were all falling down... it had a tin roof and tin sides, so everything was rather basic – the only thing they had there of brick was a brick loo... They were just dealing with wheels and carts in the usual run-of-the-mill wheelwright business. Market carts they did a number of. And they began doing, once the fashion for coach driving came in, they did work for Sir Dymoke White... they had a sewing machine in the workshop for sewing up the upholstery. (*Bernard Hoad*)

The Benham family ran a dairy business in New Road until 1955, keeping cows in a stable behind their dairy. Milk was delivered from churns carried on a horse-drawn cart, or milk float.

Well, milking, you know, always starts early. Depends on the time of the year... You always get up at daylight to start milking, don't you?... We always milked by

hand. All our lives we milked by hand. Finest machine in the world, your hand!... In that shed down there we had 33 of them [cows].... Well, you would carry as many churns as the floor of the cart would allow. Mind you, you would have to leave room for yourself to stand up and drive the horse, wouldn't you?... Anyway, if your customer wanted a pint, you would use a pint measure, if a half-pint, a half-pint measure... (*Robert Bentam, dairyman 1919–55*)

Milk was not the only thing to be sold door-to-door, So were fish, vegetables and bread. Bill Porter sold toffee apples from a stall in Charlotte Street and later from handcart.

Thursdays, Fridays, and Saturdays, down Charlotte Street for three days, then Sunday on the barrow... Always in Leigh Park, and Fareham... I bought a proper caravan affair and you could make the toffee apples in there if you wanted. That I used twice because we used to make 'em and sell them straight out at Fareham... What would I say? "Sixpence each, or fourpence each, toffee apples", in a loud voice! (*W.G. Porter, working in the 1940s–'80s.*)

And I used to do a Saturday job, for the Co-op as a baker's rounds boy... And I used to be at the bakery at half-seven in the morning and they were selling

Charlotte Street market, near Christmas 1996.

the Football Mail on Fratton Bridge when we took the horse and cart back to the Co-op in Fratton Road. Because I can recollect that the newspaper boy shouting out one night, you know, "Football Mail!" and the blasted horse reared up and we had hell to pay going up the bridge with this horse. So I worked for them for two bob on Saturday, and that really tired me out because the baker never stopped. He just ate a sandwich, and that was it. Kept on with the old bread all day long. And that was hard work when I was 14 years of age then. And I had to get a licence from the education department in Victoria Road, a badge that one had to pay sixpence for to wear so that you could carry out this two-bob-a-day baker's rounds job. (*Frank Deacon, born 1922*)

Most people got their daily needs at local shops, such as that run by Charles and Annie Barton in the late 1930s, sometimes buying a scoop of jam for a penny.

A small corner shop, general shop, open all hours, sold everything, almost everything that anyone would need. Hand-to-mouth trade, open from eight o'clock in the morning till eight o'clock at night, six-and-a-half days a week when we first went there, and that included all day Sunday, which after a while my father decided wasn't going to happen any more and he just opened for a couple of hours on Sunday morning... sweets, cigarettes, butter, margarine, lard,

Charles and Annie Barton's shop stood on the corner of Crasswell Street and Cottage View, Landport.

to the floating bridge and back to Portsmouth. (*Jim Lodge, born 1926*)

From the time I was 12 I was with my father... I used to get on my bike and go round and pick up the bets with the money. Which was illegal at the time, but hope they don't mind that now... [Mr Emery's father fell ill] And who had to take over the business, but me, at 16 years old. But my uncle Fred in Thorncroft Road, he was also a bookmaker, so he used to keep an eye on me and I carried on until about 19... So I went out and got a job, eventually, as – what shall I say – a salesman with the Hoover company... Oh yes. Door-to-door selling. Actually I started with... Electrolux. I started with them first but I couldn't get on with them because they had women canvassers, you see. You used to get these canvassings given to you to go out with and quite a lot of the time they had faked them to get their numbers up, you see. You would go to a place and it would be "I don't know what you are talking about". So I decided to pack that up and go to Hoover's. You did your own canvassing. You got £2 a week less stamp, and commission on top, you see. (*Gordon Emery, born 1914*)

Meeting the stars is very nice, of course. For example I was with Princess Irene of Greece. She was with Sir Yehudi Menuhin. They were attending a concert in the city. Performers from all over the world were attending... She asked me if she could have some of the

cheese, eggs, sugar, tea, a small range of tinned fruit and fish, patent medicines... cake, biscuits, matches, tape and elastic by the yard, buttons... soap, ladies' stockings, men's socks, the Vantas machine, of course, selling fizzy drinks... (*Marie Spraggs, née Barton*)

Other occupations got you out and about.

When I left school I went to work for Brewers as an errand boy in Marmion Road... I can even remember going from there with a cycle with tea and coffee and going across from Marmion Road down to Old Portsmouth, across on the floating bridge to Gosport, and going from Gosport right through to Lee on Solent, delivering things. Only small amounts. And then cycling back

colour photographs that I had taken, and I said that if the Lord Mayor did not send them himself I would personally deliver them. She said that I was welcome in the palace at any time. "If you should come over to Greece contact me". I thought this was very nice. I worked with Prince Andrew for three hours following him around, escorting him around the area, and he was quite cheeky to me. (*Ken Pratt, photographer from the 1940s–'90s*)

Harry Sutton on drums, with his band, about 1950.

Working in music was often supplemented by regular jobs. George Bennett led the Carlton Dance Band on Clarence Pier for seven years from 1924-5, and then played naval establishments, while Harry Sutton, a travelling salesman for Bovril, led a series of bands in the 1930s–'50s.

He had a day job as well. He was with the Hampshire Furnishing Co daytime, and he had the bands at night. He had two or three bands out, sometimes, years ago, but he has always been musically minded, that was the thing that he liked best. (*Kathleen Lewis & Cynthia Cobb, George Bennett's daughters*)

... about eight o'clock climb in his car with his brief case and he would just drive off and he had a journey and he'd go round and he'd make those calls on that day and the next day he would do different calls in another different area. In other words he had a four-week cycle of daily

journeys... Occasionally as telephones became more and more popular quite a few people used to phone through and say "Oh is Harry there?" Everybody knew my father as Harry or Mr Bovril... Mostly dance band music. That was his basic forte. The dance band was sort of, in those days it was like the modern pop music of the day. I mean in those days you had melody and beat to it and you could even hear the words and understand them. (*Derek Sutton*)

When Jack Price's father died in 1927 leaving a widow and two young sons, the family had to work hard to make ends meet.

So my mother was just left with the widow's pension, which I believe was about 10s 6d. I can't remember whether there was a piece on that – extra – for me. She was still supporting me. So she started to take in laundry and

I used to have to go and get it and take it back. She used to get up at 4 o'clock in the morning and light the copper which was built in in the house – coal-fired. She would do the washing, she would dry it round the fire or in the garden if the weather was clement. She would iron it or mangle it, whichever, and then I would take it back again. So we ran a virtually 24-hour laundry

Jack Price in his telegraph boy uniform, aged 16.

service in those days. Additionally, I took on a newspaper round with W.H. Smith who had a shop in Albert Road at the time.

Migrants to Portsmouth from overseas have often established themselves in the catering trade. They have included Swiss, Italians (Albertolli's, Verrecchia's), Chinese and, since the 1960s, Bangladeshis, who own most of the 'Indian' restaurants in the city.

In Portsmouth, he [the interviewee's brother] set up a restaurant, he was working before with the airlines, travel agent and since then, when he came to Portsmouth, he had a business, that's why he came. His wife was teacher, she was teaching at a

Slicing onions in the kitchen of the Gandhi restaurant, 2002.

Portsmouth school. And somehow, they managed to come to Portsmouth and I followed them... It is part of family, when I was working with him I became a partner, a working partner. Since then I've been working in a catering business of my own... I had my own business in Fareham, I was also working for some other businesses... Eventually I got my own business with a couple of partners in Fareham. From there, I had another business... I bought a business in Milton Road, Portsmouth that I run for about ten years. (*Bangladeshi restaurateur*)

Well it's traditionally, yes it is curry, but you got to be fitted with Western palate because you cannot serve old traditional food to somebody who's never been eating curry or that food before... It's not much different – slightly – because if I cook at home the flavour would be slightly stronger, doesn't mean to be hot... more spicy flavour... We use the same spice, same everything at the home, same spice at the restaurant but quantity is the difference... [serving alcohol] Well as a Muslim it's against the rule because we don't [drink] alcohol. European people do not eat anything [without drinking alcohol] – very rare you find people not drinking alcohol, so if we don't have alcohol in the restaurant then we very few customer we'll get in the restaurant... if you want to do the restaurant business then you got to, you have no alternative if

you want to make it a success. (*Muhammed Badruzzaman, restaurateur*)

The late 20th century has brought new occupations. Philip Wrixton left school 1972 and joined IBM. His career has been marked by its variety, typical of modern computing and electronics. In the first 15 years, for example:

I started in the Havant branch, can't remember how many years I was there, quite a few in fact, and then I moved down to Northern Road, which is now, I think, the tax office building in Cosham, which was meant to be a temporary building for IBM, for just a few years. When I moved down there again I was working in the computer centre, but more in networking. I started to travel at that point, as well and went all over the UK installing some of the very early telecommun-ications systems that were appearing at that time. From there I moved on to a job in North Harbour, which was then being built, and actually set up the whole infrastructure of data processing, data communications which was being moved across from other centres... (*Philip Wrixton, left school at 18 in 1972*)

I see directors, I see – with my job, the good thing about it is I see people from all levels of life – to director level – to people who are chefs on and off – and it's very varied. The job I do, I see people from all walks of life, people such as you doing research and part of my job is to do training within Portsmouth College and Highbury College, give people training awareness. I do a lot of presentations. Last Friday I was in Chichester giving a presentation to Chichester Council members. From the Chief Executives to the housing officers, everyone attended. We did four sessions which involved nearly 200 people. (*Rumal Khan, business adviser*).

One of the boats used to ferry animals and vehicles to the Isle of Wight before the first roll-on-roll-off ferry service in 1928.

Transport

There have always been a great variety of types of transport in Portsmouth. Although bicycles were already widely used by 1900, trains, horsebuses, trams and the trolleybuses and motorbuses that replaced them were all important to the city's inhabitants. The oldest form of transport is perhaps the boats that ferried people across the harbour or over to the Isle of Wight.

They were taking a circus over to the Isle of Wight. Well, they used to take them on the old tow-boats. They used to be a big, blunt-prowed thing, and they used to have a drop at the back that they put down and it made a pontoon for them to go up into it... They take three in a line and they had a smart blue steam tug, the *Adur*, and that used to tow them across to Wooton Creek and land them there. (*Eileen Rayner, resident of Point before 1914*)

Horses were the main motive power in 1900, and needed much time to look after.

First of all you had to feed him straightaway. Not market morning, you didn't have time to feed him market mornings, when you brought him home he had his breakfast... the other days of course you had to clean him, brush him down. Sometimes they laid on their own manure and if you had a coloured horse he was all brown and you had to wash him down before you went out with him and took him out on the round and that. It was just an automatic way of life then. (*Harry Cullimore, greengrocer and coal merchant, born 1900*)

Driver and conductor overcoated against the cold, about 1910.

Up until shortly before World War Two, a May Day parade was held through the streets of Portsmouth. Most businesses contributed a float.

All the horses were decorated with ribbons and wool, and God-knows-what, and feathers and the rest of it. And all the traders' carts were all specially painted up brand new for it, and of course there was this parade.... They used to congregate in Alexandra Park, in North End... everybody would be lined up on both sides of the road to see it go by. (*Robert Benham, dairyman 1919–55*)

Between 1903 and 1935 there was a tramway system from

Cosham to Horndean, the Portsdown & Horndean Light Railway. By 1930 it was suffering from competition from motorbuses. Louis Bushill joined it at 17.

The rate of pay was 6d an hour for junior conductors; that's up to the age of 21, and 8d an hour for over 21 and 9d an hour for drivers. Well, a driver had to be 21. Now to save that 2d an hour they took roughly nine of us, as far as I can remember, all on there at once. Now they put us all on the trams – we didn't get paid for the tuition – they put us on a fortnight's tuition on the regular trams, with normal conductors, to learn the ropes. Then, as soon as we passed out as conductors, they sacked the

chaps as was teaching us. You can't hardly imagine that, but it's absolutely true... When it was our turn to be 21 we were due for the sack: some did get the sack, but fortunately for me they had a post for a tram driver.

In the inter-war period horses were displaced by motor vehicles; at Campions they were phased out by 1939.

Campions had horses and carts to deliver their products. Campions, I think, were first in the city to fit pneumatic tyres to their baker's carts. This had advantages for quietness, but I think was probably more difficult for the horses to pull... That was the early introduction of the Morrison electrics... For the

Cyril Stares with the lorry he drove in the late 1920s, bringing milk from the countryside for Street's, the first dairy in Portsmouth to sell bottled milk.

domestic deliveries within the radius... of the bakery, lets say it was five to seven miles, there was this gradual policy of replacing the petrol vehicles with the Morrison electrics. (*David Miles, son of Campions' managing director*)

Even in 1939 motor vehicles still presented a physical challenge.

At the beginning of the war I changed my job and went over to Timothy White's. I changed it because for the last eight years I'd been driving a 12-ton wagon and in fact it was beginning to hurt my back. On that 12-ton wagon there was no self-starter, you had to start it all by a great handle on the front. And it used to take two of us to turn the engine over to start it and I was beginning to feel that my back was beginning to strain. (*Cyril Stares, lorry and bus driver, 1920s-'60s*)

In the 1960s, running council buses was regarded as man's work.

...there were no women hired except those which had lasted from the war period. I think I am right in saying that the corporation had an active policy of not hiring women in the 1960s, to be conductors or drivers. There were no women drivers left when I was on there, the last driver had packed in a fair few number of years before, but there were about six or seven women conductors who were survivors from the 1939-45

Diana Hart-Thomas (right) and her colleague Sylvia, stewardesses for Channel Airways, 1962.

period. Try that in 1997! [the date of his interview] (*Paul Stoneham, conductor in the late 1960s*)

One totally new form of transport appeared in the course of the century – air travel

Then I decided that life was leaving me behind and polished up my French and became an air hostess, starting in Portsmouth. We had an airport then, up on Eastern Road, now a housing estate. I started there with Channel Airways, flying to the Channel Islands and Paris... there was no restriction on hours for cabin crew in those days. If you complained, as I remember we did once at Channel Airways, about the number of hours we were working, from sun up to sun down in the summer season, we were just told that there were lots of other girls out there hanging on hooks waiting for these jobs. (*Diana Hart-Thomas, stewardess in the early 1960s*)

Trades unions

Attitudes to trade unions have always differed widely. Union power was weak before 1939, but strong in the 1960s and '70s. Portsmouth Corporation Tramways were largely unionised and its staff supported the miners during the General Strike of 1926.

... we never stopped running, we must have continued on into the town much to the annoyance of the corporation, I suppose, as they came out on strike, lots and lots of them lost their jobs because after a time the

corporation said anyone who doesn't turn up by 10 o'clock on a certain day will be declared redundant, or whatever they called it in those days. (*Fred Eames, conductor on the Portsdown & Horndean Light Railway*)

And my dad was very active and of course, being an activist, he was practised against. He was practiced against – because he would go around and 'preach' to the people about the advantages of binding together, combining their assets both physical and financial, and being after to protect one another... When he came back to work after he had this – the first incident with this ulcer – he was sent to take over the district of Paulsgrove and Wymering on a bicycle. If you have suffered a gastric ulcer and been subject to haemorrhages of the stomach, one doesn't expect to find oneself relegated to the most hilly borough in the city.

But that is what happened to him. (*Frank Deacon, whose father was a supervisor in the council's cleansing dept in the 1960s*)

In the early 1960s the council introduced one-man buses.

The union was strong then, because when we started the one-man system the union wouldn't have it, because they could see that they had done away with conductors. They were union men. The firm wouldn't have sacked 'em anyway. They would have found them a job, but, at any rate, for six months the one-man buses were in the shed while they were arguing about getting them on the road. (*Louis Bushill, an inspector in the 1960s*)

The corset factories unionised slowly.

It was the Tailors and Garment Workers Union... I managed to get the girls to join and it was a good thing because... they were even covered and, if they had an accident at work, you know, with the machines or anything like that. And finally they agreed to have the union in and the bosses said, "yes you can have the..." It was, it was okay as regards that we were covered for accidents and things like that, but it didn't alter much about the pay. I mean, I have gone up to London to union headquarters and I have been there all day and we have argued and argued and talked and talked and I have come back with a penny. A penny on the hour. And this is how it was in those days, it was poor pay. (*Etta*

One-man operation in Highland Road, about 1965.

The last Trident fuselage to be built at De Havilland's factory in Portsmouth, which closed shortly after.

Cook, machinist and supervisor at Twilfits, 1935–80)

There was a union, we had a union at Leethems and you paid sixpence or a shilling a week for the union and then if anything went wrong, I mean like we weren't happy with the prices, you would go to the union if we didn't go on strike. (*Doreen Kemp, flat binder, 1945–99*)

I can remember being out on strike, yes, standing at the gate, what the hell it was for I haven't

got a clue, quite frankly, 'cos you never gain out of strikes in any case. We had various strikes at one time or another, I mean sometimes you didn't agree with them, but I mean, being unionised that was the question, you were out and that was it. (*L. Munden, joined Airspeed in 1936, talking of a strike in 1957–58*)

When there were massive redundancies at the Airspeed factory in 1961 the unions were:

Submissive, really, it's the only word to describe it. You know, you got the usual furore in the first few hours, but the inevitability, the totality, really of the move just defeated them, there was nothing they could do. There was no support from other units in the group... because apart from Hawker Siddeley's the entire aircraft industry was facing the same problem... (*Chris Townsley*)

PORTSMOUTH DOCKYARD IN THE 20TH CENTURY:

CONTINUITY, CHANGE AND CLOSURE

Ken Lunn and Ann Day

Introduction: only left with memories

The role of British royal dockyards is primarily the repair and maintenance of the Royal Navy's ships, coupled with the construction of new vessels when required (between 1900 and 1960, 47 vessels were built in Portsmouth dockyard). Portsmouth became effectively the first naval dockyard in Britain when a dry dock was constructed in 1495. During the first half of the 20th century, the dockyard in Portsmouth was central to its economy and had a major impact on employment patterns in the town. There are very few Portsmouth people in

The Main Gate, HM Dockyard, c.1910

their 70s or 80s who have either not worked in the dockyard at some time in their lives, or who do not know someone who was a dockyard worker.

The history of the yard, however, is not an even one. Its fortunes have been closely related to the needs of the navy and the demands of British foreign policy. Expansion and contraction, lay-offs and peaks of employment have been a constant. Total numbers employed in 1900 were approximately 10,000, increasing to 16,500 by the outbreak of war in 1914. Indeed, demands for workers during World War One were so high that women were recruited to undertake work previously done by men. The 1920s, however, were a period of massive reductions in both shipbuilding construction and employment levels. Numbers of workers in Portsmouth dockyard in the mid-1920s had decreased back to their pre-1914 total of approximately 12,000. It was not until the mid-1930s, and a policy of rearmament, that the work-force began to increase again, reaching its highest level during World War Two with over 25,000 workers. Women workers were again mobilised for dockyard work and contributed to the war effort in nearly every department.

The post-war period has again seen considerable changes in the dockyard, firstly in the rapid decrease in employment numbers from the 1960s, and also in the more recent change of its role from a naval dockyard to that of a naval base. Privatisation of many services has also been a feature of these years, resulting in the complete handing over of naval base services to private ownership in 1998, and the reduction of the workforce to 1,500. These major changes, coupled with new technologies and different shipbuilding techniques, have resulted in the loss of numerous trades and skills and, perhaps most importantly, the loss of a particular work culture that has left Portsmouth with only memories of its dockyard past.

Apprenticeship and training: 'a battle for survival' or 'a golden opportunity'?

There were a number of ways that men and women could gain entry into the dockyard world, but the main openings for tradesmen and clerical workers were governed by the dockyard and civil service examinations.

For the craftsman, a dockyard examination, which was held in all the dockyard towns, was taken at the age of 15 or 16. The pass mark determined what you were... the higher your marks were, the greater chance you had. The electricians were the elite trades [in the 1940s], then the engine fitters and the shipwrights, although at the end of the day it was the shipwrights, really, that had the best opportunities, because the first two or three in the Dockyard School went on to Greenwich to be ship constructors. (*Cyril Rutter, engine fitter apprentice, 1942–47*)

For working-class families, the Dockyard School education was really an absolute godsend because very few people could get to university then, even if they were bright enough, unless you got a state scholarship. It was a golden opportunity for those willing and able to take it. (*Keith Thomas, shipwright apprentice, 1939–44, later Ship Constructor and Director of Dockyards*)

Women clerks in the Constructive Dept, March 1917.

Shipwright apprentices working on HMS *Sylvana*.

I filled in a form [for the dockyard] and luckily I was called in for an interview and took what was then a short answer test... and I managed to scrape through, and I started in the September of 1972 as a clerical assistant, as they were then. (*Valerie Willis, clerical assistant, 1972–93*)

We were not really trained... you were first put on a section and worked under somebody for a few weeks and then you were on your own. As you rose up the ranks, you were put in charge of other girls who had come into the job. (*Mrs Nora Callan, clerical assistant, 1927–37*)

As pointed out earlier, employment in the dockyard was not always easy to obtain, particularly during the Depression of the late 1920s.

It was such a bad state... apprentices were coming out of their time, coming out as journeymen for two weeks and then being given the sack. But there was nothing outside, so you took your five-year apprenticeship, if you could get it, and knew that you got three years schooling as well. (*Frederick Chick, shipwright apprentice 1930–35*)

The outbreak of World War Two led to an increased demand for apprentices and a subsequent change in recruiting strategies.

A notice came offering yardboys the chance to sit a supplementary examination for apprenticeships, because the numbers from the normal entry of apprenticeships into the dockyard had not come up to the numbers they required. We went to the Dockyard School, which in those days was in the dockyard itself, and we sat this exam on a Saturday morning. We started at nine in the morning and I was back indoors for half-past ten, so it was a real stiff one! On the Monday morning the results came out and I'd come top. (*Ernest Horn, yardboy 1940*)

Although shipwrights continued to dominate the dockyard managerial structure, new apprentices were increasingly turning to

the electrical and engineering trades as opportunities outside the dockyard widened in these areas. A dilution scheme was initiated in an effort to alleviate the problems of recruiting shipwright apprentices. Workmen from the junior trades, such as welders, caulkers and boilermakers, were allowed to take up a trade apprenticeship.

After the war they started taking dilutee mechanics. What happened, Vospers [a local shipbuilding company] were paying more money than the dockyard and the youngsters went out in droves... boilermakers and all the different trades, so they were short of mechanics. They brought in a dilution scheme and what happened, if you were accepted, you did six years' instructional training and I went in as a shipwright. When you finished that, they gave you a certificate to say that you had served that time and they recognised you as a shipwright. But unfortunately, I did 5 years and 6 months, because they stopped the scheme when trained mechanics started to come back into the dockyard, so had to go back to my original trade as a boilermaker. (*William Pinch, shipwright apprentice, 1953–58*)

The wartime period also changed recruitment policies for women clerical workers, not only increasing their number through the introduction of temporary clerical assistants, but by

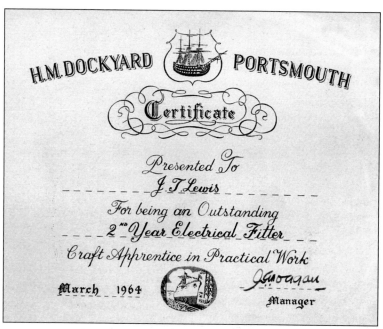

Certificate presented to electrical fitter apprentice, J.T. Lewis, for outstanding practical work.

allowing greater flexibility in their promotion. After the war civil service examinations were re-instated and a number of temporary clerical assistants were given permanent posts.

Before the war the higher jobs were always taken by men, Higher Clerical Officers and above... women didn't get promoted above Clerical Officer until later. (*Mrs Nora Callan, clerical assistant 1927–37*)

I went in during the war in the stores and they had stopped the exams then. At the end of the war there was an interview board... you could apply to be put forward to the board for an interview for promotion, and that's how I became a Clerical Officer. That was quite a time... after the end of the war. I was more or less in charge of a

section. (*Mrs Barbara Pitman, clerical officer, 1940–54*)

The first experiences of dockyard life were sometimes overwhelming, particularly for the young men and women who came straight from school and had no previous experience of the dockyard environment.

I can remember my first day there, I was nearly in tears at the end of the day... everything was strange and different and I just wanted to get home. By the second day they started to give us tasks to do and then you just got on with it. I remember the first task they gave us to do, they gave us, I think it was an inch-and-a-half diameter and four inches long of mild steel, a hammer, chisel and files, and you were expected, with a cold chisel and hammer, to make this lump of mild steel into a square and then file it square into an inch square. At the end of the week your hands were all sort of bruised and bloodied and I can remember I had bits of old handkerchief around my hands, but by the end of the week you had learnt to hit the chisel and not your hand... it was all part of a training exercise! (*Edward Saunders, engine fitter apprentice 1941–46*)

When I first went in there I was overwhelmed... I've never seen so many men popping up from holes in the walls and holes in the ground and I thought, oh dear, I'm not going to like this. (*Mrs R Hooper, woman worker 1941*)

The first two years of my apprenticeship were in actual fact more a battle for survival than learning a trade, because there were some pretty hard cases in there. (*Mr D. Hill, shipwright apprentice, 1940–45*)

A number of people who were in the dockyard for most of their working lives talk about the changes in apprenticeships and training procedures.

A lot of things were handed down, not taken from a book or off a piece of paper, it was handed down and that's been from years and years... and you pick it up and carry on... and it's a short cut to a lot of things because the experience has been handed down to you. (*William Pinch, boilermaker, 1959–83*)

The 240-ton crane, Portsmouth dockyard, 1959–60.

After the war they had a Training Centre and all the apprentices did their first two years together there. It was divided into two sections. One was between No.8 and No.11 Dock, at the end of the old Light Plate Shop, and it was called the Shipwrights' Apprentice Training Centre. You spent three months on every section and there was probably about 30 boys in my group. (*Brian Patterson, shipwright 1950–93*)

The old Dockyard School was bombed in 1941 and classes were moved to the Teacher's Training College at Milton. After the war a temporary training centre was built

HMS *Tiger* in the dockyard, 1959–60.

outside Unicorn Gate, with the school then moving to Flathouse Quay, until a new purpose-built training centre was established (later taken over by Highbury College).

After this they built us some Nissen huts by the Unicorn Gate, and these were quite good. There were eight huts with specially-built labs and so on. We were then offered the old Mechanical Repair Establishment (naval) at Flathouse, and we took over the teaching part there... we were there until 1970 when it was handed over to the polytechnic and Highbury College. That was the end of the Dockyard School... the old order had changed and it was a sad time for me to see the end of what was a wonderful system for a lot of people. (*Ernest George, schoolmaster and principal, 1937–74*)

As part of re-planning strategies from the 1970s, apprenticeships were short-ened to four years (later to three years) and initial train-ing encompassed all three of the main trades, mechanical, electrical and engineering.

In the first year we were in the Unicorn Training Centre doing machining and fitting, mostly benchwork, and we went to Highbury one day a week for the City & Guilds certificate. We don't go into the dockyard until the second year and it's only a three-year apprenticeship now. (*Andrew Flux, mechanical apprentice, 1997–2000*)

A female apprentice signwriting for HMS *Dryad*. (By courtesy of *The News*)

It is one of the best apprenticeships, definitely in the South... you do such a variety of jobs. For the first six months you don't even do your own trade, you do all the three trades... mechanical, electrical and constructive. You can do your job more efficiently if you understand what everyone else has to do, that is the thinking behind it. (*Sarah Nicholson, electrical apprentice, 1995–98*)

In 1969, craft apprenticeships in Portsmouth dockyard were opened for the first time to women. Taking them up has not always been an easy process, as the following extracts reveal.

When I first started there was so much emphasis on sexual

harrassment and equality... because the Training Officer was keen for the girls to do as well as the boys, but on the other hand, you are constantly having to prove that you can do the job, at least as well as the boys. (*Donna Sadler, mechanical apprentice, 1994–98*)

There was one particular lecturer who turned round to me and the other girl [apprentice] and said "Do you know you've taken apprenticeships away from two lads?" and that was his attitude. (*Sarah Nicholson, electrical apprentice, 1995–98*)

I started my apprenticeship as an electrical fitter in 1973. There weren't many opportunities for women in electrical work elsewhere and I was able to specialise as an electrician maintaining the dockyard buildings and plant. I enjoy my work, it's varied and most of the men treat me with respect because I know what I'm doing. (*Ros Goller, Electrical Fitter, 1973–present*)

One of the main changes in relations between young workers and their instructors or supervisors was the level of formality, and this was the same for both men and women.

It was quite strict discipline then, you couldn't stop and chat because the chap in charge would tell you to get on with your work. It was always "Miss", they never used Christian names in those days... the men were always

"Mr So-and-so" and it was quite formal. (*Mrs J. Deluchi, clerical assistant, 1936–47*)

The foreman was God Almighty in those days. You didn't even call your chargeman by his Christian name, he was always "Mr". (*Mr D. Hill, shipwright apprentice, 1940–45*)

I always called my instructor "Mr" during the whole of my training time with him. I knew his Christian name, but I never called him by it. Mind you, some of the apprentices were less respectful and used to have nicknames for their instructors. Our instructor had a head of white hair and a big white moustache, so one apprentice always referred to him as 'the shepherd from the hills' [he was a plumber and carried a long piece of wire for measuring up, which looked like a shepherd's crook]. (*Thomas Lee, plumber, 1933–82*)

During and after World War Two, this formality was relaxed a little, although workers were still aware of the management hierarchy.

We called our instructor Bert... but you were still expected to get on with your work and the instructors made sure that the boys could pass their trade tests. (*Cyril Rutter, engine fitter apprentice 1942–47*)

Types of work: 'on bread and dripping, feet and inches, we've built battleships'

Up to the late 1960s, the dockyard workforce was divided into five different departments – Manager Constructive Department (MCD); Manager Engineering Department (MED); Electrical Engineering Manager (EEM); Navy Works Department (later the Civil Engineering Department); and Captain of the Port Department. Once a man had entered the dockyard, either through an apprenticeship, as a yardboy,

Laying the keel of HMS *Dreadnought*.

Launching a Dreadnought battleship.

as a dilutee, through the Labour Exchange, or by transferring from another dockyard, he was allocated to one of the five dockyard departments and to a particular section of that department. After a period of time (which varied according to employment demands) a man could become established, which entitled him to pension rights and, provided he did not infringe any of the dockyard regulations, to a 'job for life'. It is impossible to give examples of all the trades and jobs in the dockyard, but the following extracts provide a flavour of the huge variety of skills that were required in the servicing of the naval fleet over the course of the 20th century.

... there weren't many professions that you couldn't find in the dockyard... from all the heavy industrial ones such as the founder, the ship fitter, engine fitter, the patternworker, and then backing these up would be your French polisher, your sailmakers, laggers, all the different branches of your electrical fitters, joiners, drillers, caulkers, riveters. It was thought in the old days that you needed the labour there to service the fleet. (*Brian Patterson, shipwright, 1950–95*)

I went into the dockyard as an iron moulder in the Foundry. It involved making castings of all descriptions – iron, brass, steel – for the ships, pipes, rudders... you use a wooden pattern [from the Patternmakers Shop] of the object you are going to produce and from that you make a sand mould, into which the metal is poured. The Foundry was in three sections, an iron foundry at one end, the brass foundry and then a smaller brass foundry, then there was a steel foundry, the only one in the whole of the MOD, so they did quite a lot of work for Vosper Thornycroft. (*Arthur Matthews, foundryman, 1933*)

Ship work was vastly different to shop work... but it was surprising, you could not get people to come into the shops from afloat, because they were under surveillance all the time, so even though the conditions on ship were terrible – cold, dirty, dangerous, heavy work – some men preferred the relative freedom of the ships. (*Ernest Horn, shipwright, 1940–89*)

I took a junior apprenticeship during the war and when I got into it I realised that it was a pretty tough job... they used to rivet the ships then rather than weld them, as they do now. Basically what you done, you went with a riveter and he would let you have a go at knocking down a rivet. The rivets were heated on a forge and thrown to the riveter by a 'dollyholder'. It was noisy work with all the hammers going. (*Ron Bartlett, riveter, 1944–90*)

I spent a number of years on the Mould Loft floor. This is where they used to lay ships off on the floor to get the shape of moulds and that sort of thing... of course, it's all done on computers nowadays. (*Mr. D Hill, shipwright, 1940–89*)

A system of Planning and Progress was introduced in the 1960s with the aim of improving efficiency by bringing the whole productive system under the central control of a general manager. Whilst the three main departments remained intact (MCD, EEM and MED), all planning and production had to be implemented through a tightly-controlled administrative process. There was an accompanying change in job titles and style of work. Chargemen, inspectors and foremen became Professional Technical Officers (PTOs), graded from IV to I as they were promoted through the ranks.

As a Constructor-in-Charge you basically had charge of an element of the workforce... I was in overall charge of the construction of HMS *Sirius* in 1960. It was at that time that a thing called 'Network Scheduling' was just beginning to make its appearance felt... it was a very logical, analytical system of planning... it identified the critical points of the project. (*Keith Thomas, Constructor-in-Charge, 1960*)

Progress and Planning, as they called it, the system, apparently, what they adopted in the dockyard was tried in America and was found to be no good,

Dockyard workers making a mast.

but they made it work in there... but it wasn't any good. A lot of the problem being that in the early days, the old days, you had people that were experienced and the experience was handed down, so you come across a problem and I could say to the inspector, right, we'd have the answer to it straight away, but as time went by, the people we had then would have to get in touch with Bath, so by the time we got the answer back, could be a couple of weeks. (*W.C. Harris, shipwright, 1952–90*)

You organised your work so that you were getting on with

something else [while waiting for a part of a job to be done elsewhere, such as machining, drilling or welding]... you organised a flow of work through the different chargeman. When they brought in planning, that all changed. (*Thomas Lee, plumber, 1933–81*)

The planning of how the ship would be constructed was like this... I had a Mechanical Department Inspector, a Constructive Department Inspector and an Electrical Inspector and there was a Yard Planning Officer and a Ship Planning Officer. The Yard

Planning Officer did the preparatory work for when the ship was built from the keel up in one of the docks, and the Ship Planning Officer then took over for the rest of the construction... it was very professional and they trained their officers to a good standard. (*Ray Hayhoe, electrical fitter/inspector/Senior PTO, 1944–88*)

Well, when we went over to metric, that was really great! My first metric measurement I looked at, I thought it was the date! A mate of mine, a shipwright, he ordered some wood screws... but by the time it went through the

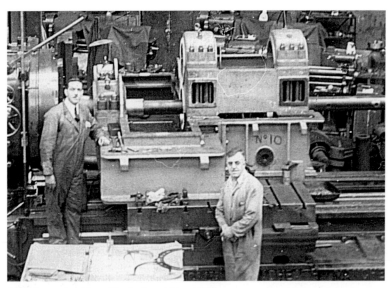

Bill Butler, engine fitter, with a boring machine c.1965.

National Service after the war had a terrific impact on apprentices in the dockyard... they came out of their time, did their two years and a lot of them didn't come back... quite a number of them did quite well for themselves in other jobs... a lot went into the Merchant Navy. (*Dennis Puddick, engine fitter apprentice, 1948–53*)

Women workers: 'just a gaggle of women'

The dockyard has long been regarded as the domain of men and, for a large part of the 20th century, this was indeed the case. However, a small number of women worked in the Colour Loft making flags, canvas bags and overalls, and these workers were mostly widows of naval and dockyard personnel. It was not until World War One that women were employed in jobs which had previously been defined as men's work, but in 1919 women were quickly replaced by men returning from the war.

Planning Office, being metric, a lorry turned up with thousands of wood screws... it was a lorry load! The old hands used to say, "What do we want this for?... on bread and dripping, feet and inches, we've built battleships". (*W. C. Harris, shipwright, 1952–90*)

The post-war period also saw changes in opportunities for employment outside of the dockyard, which began to affect recruitment demands.

In the 1960s there were terrible labour problems because, with the ordinary labourers, we used to have critical shortages because of the seasonal trade... during the summer months the casual labourers would just take themselves out of the dockyard and get jobs in the holiday industry, where they would get much more pay and then would clamour to come back in the winter months. The other problem was electrical fitters,

because after the war there was a lot of development of local industries and there was quite a need, particularly in the electrical industries. They were taking electrical fitters from the dockyard who were being put into white overalls and much better conditions with better pay. (*Keith Thomas, Ship Constructor/Chief Executive, 1939–84*)

Dockyard workers using Marc Brunel's blockmaking machinery, 1970s.

Women were employed in working lathes, planes, milling, engraving, buffing, auto and slotting machinery; and in cleaning, cutting and testing condenser tubes; making condenser ferrules, and cleaning air bottles for submarines and ships; in general bench work and assisting the mechanics in cutting blades for condenser turbines. In the Boiler Shop they were engaged in acetylene welding and cleaning, picking, galvanising and testing boiler tubes. (*Extract from Recollections, film on women in Portsmouth dockyard during the World War One*)

My father was in the navy and he went down on HMS *Victoria* in June 1893. He was only 26 and mother had a pension from the Victoria Fund and from the Admiralty. I worked in a corset factory as a machinist and went into the dockyard in 1917 and worked in the Block Mills. (*Valence Stubbs, block maker, 1917–19*)

I went into the Torpedo Shop [as a packer]... you had boxes and you had all the parts [of a torpedo] that you had to count, put back in the boxes, and then they went back into the Stores... Mrs Sullivan was our supervisor, she was very stern! (*Mrs Nellie Richards, torpedo packer, 1916–19*)

I went into the dockyard in the Electrical Department [EED] in the Armature Shop. We started at seven in the morning and often worked overtime until seven at night. When we first started I got a pound a week, which was quite good money then... by 1919 I was getting £3 a week. We were trained by the skilled men working on magneto coils on a machine... all the girls did different work, some on large size coils and some did soldering work as well. The men did the very heavy work, the huge armatures for the ships. (*Daisy Purvin, armature winder, 1916–19*)

The men were not always willing to accept working alongside women and some were very scathing about their capabilities. However, others were surprised to find that many women were able to do very heavy work and were not afraid to undertake the many tasks that had previously been viewed as 'men's' work.

Every smith has a striker and during the war [World War One] I had a woman allotted to me... by God she could use a seven-pound hammer! I taught the girls how to use a soldering iron... I told them when you go round to the toilet for heaven's sake wash your hands first, else you'll wonder what's biting you... sodium zinc chloride, if it gets on your hands it leaves little black spots, and they itch like hell! (*Bill Levett, locksmith, 1904–c.1950*)

Woman dockyard worker in World War One, showing overalls, boots and triangle badge.

We wore brown overalls and a cap, with boots because of the cobbled floors. They also had a triangle badge saying 'On War Work' and we were sometimes called the 'triangle girls'. (*Valence Stubbs, woman worker, 1917–19*)

We felt proud to wear that badge, because we were doing war work. (*Daisy Purvin, woman worker, 1916–19*)

During the inter-war years, a number of women were employed in the different departments of the dockyard as clerical assistants and typists, as canteen workers and cleaners, and a few worked in the Drawing Office as tracers. During this period, more and more women were brought into non-industrial types of employment, although the civil service practised a marriage bar.

They had a marriage bar... in fact there was a great uproar one day because one of the clerical assistants was discovered to have secretly got married, and you'd have thought she had committed a crime, there was such a lot of talk about it... and, of course, she had to leave immediately. (*Mrs J.B. Deluchi, clerical assistant, 1936–47*)

Although there was no marriage bar after the war, it was still difficult for married women to get promotion to Executive Officer, or higher, because you had to be mobile and ready to move wherever you were sent... and that was not always easy if

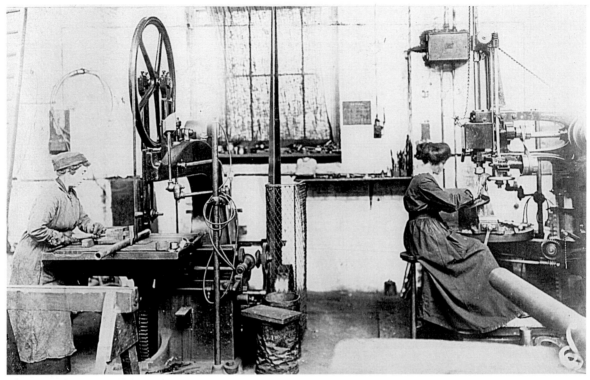

Female dockyard workers in World War One.

your husband had a job here. (*Mrs Grace Tallack, clerical officer/executive officer, 1938–78*)

One of the main areas of employment for clerical workers was in the Expense Accounts Office, where the wages for the whole dockyard were worked out.

When we first went in, they'd actually – in that office [Expense Accounts] – they'd just started using punched cards and I think this is why they were taking girls in then. I don't quite know when it started... but it must have really been in its infancy, like computers really, and we were taken in to punch the tabulating cards, they were called then, on a little hand machine. They then

went through sorting machines... which gave you a printout... it was all to do with the pay... you had the men's dockyard number and every job was coded, so you punched in the code numbers... as things progressed you can see how computers came in. (*Mrs R.D. Turner, clerical assistant, 1933*)

I was interested in becoming a tracer and I went to a school run by a Mr Tucker... it was half a crown a lesson and I was only earning 12s 6d a week at Timothy White's [a retail chemist's company]. I took an exam to become a tracer and I went into the Drawing Office. We would trace drawings onto linen... we had big drawing pins and heavy weights to stretch the linen onto a board... you pinned

the draughtsman's drawing onto the board with the linen over the top and traced the drawing with ink. These were then made into blueprints. (*Mrs Stella Threlkeld, tracer, 1936–47*)

As pointed out earlier, it was the wartime period that saw the greatest number of women entering the dockyard – to a peak of 3,000 in 1943. Although initial recruitment was through voluntary schemes, this did not produce sufficient workers and conscription was introduced in 1942 for women between the ages of 18 and 40, without dependents, who were requested to register at their local Labour Exchange and then mobilised into the

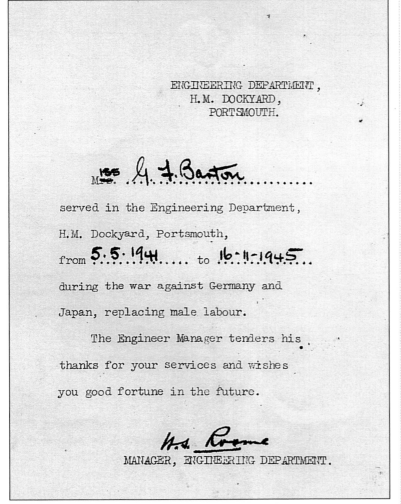

ENGINEERING DEPARTMENT,
H.M. DOCKYARD,
PORTSMOUTH.

M̶r̶s̶ .....*G. F. Barton*............

served in the Engineering Department,

H.M. Dockyard, Portsmouth,

from **5.5.1941**..... to **16.11.1945**...

during the war against Germany and

Japan, replacing male labour.

The Engineer Manager tenders his

thanks for your services and wishes

you good fortune in the future.

MANAGER, ENGINEERING DEPARTMENT.

Letter to Miss G. F. Barton, engaged on war work 1941–45.

good instructor and to become a skilled splicer you had to be able to splice a two-inch wire and then you were classed as skilled and you got the appropriate money, but not the same as the men. (*Mrs Ann Fibbins, wire splicer, 1942–45*)

When I got my call-up papers the lady said, "What would you like to be... a shipwright, an electrician or a welder?", so I stood there and I wondered in a flash which was the cleanest of the lot, and I said, er... electrician. (*Mrs Eileen Pitman, electrician's mate, 1942–46*)

The presence of women was again not always welcomed by the male workers, nor the trades unions, but their own experiences show that they felt a sense of pride in their work and a camaraderie with their colleagues.

They [the men] didn't like us, used to shout at us, tell us to be quiet... but you couldn't keep a woman quiet from talking and laughing! (*Mrs Ann Fibbins, wire splicer, 1942–45*)

The dockyard wasn't a place for genteel ways and the unions were reluctant to bring us women in because of the conditions, but I think they were worried about their jobs as well. (*Mrs Frances Trows-dale, sawmill worker, 1940–45*)

They got upset, of course, when the war ended and they had to go and make room for the men coming back. (*Ernest Horn, shipwright, 1940–89*)

munitions factories, into the forces and into the dockyards.

When I went into the dockyard you had to go in your designated gate [there were five gates at that time, the Main Gate, Unicorn, Marlborough, Anchor and East Gates] so that you could be recognised by the Recorder. I did yard clearance, just cleaning up the dockside. My chargeman said, "You're too nice a young girl to do that, how would you like to work for me?" This was doing

acetylene burning. There was no training, you just went with an older woman who showed you what to do. The job involved taking things apart [with the burner] and making them into man-handling sizes. Once I burnt a rudder from a submarine by mistake that had to be put on a ship the next day! (*Mrs Rita Rose, Engineering Workshop, 1941–46*)

I was put onto ropes at first [in the Rigging House], which I liked, and then onto wires. I had a

The Semaphore Tower burnt down in 1913 and was rebuilt in the late 1920s.

We worked in one room... it was very cramped. (*Mrs Hilda Mooney, colour loft worker, 1953–75*)

Employment for women as clerical workers increased considerably in the 1950s and '60s, with an accompanying expansion of promotion opportunities.

I took an exam and got in as a clerical assistant in the stores... it was all women workers. Later on I took the Clerical Officer's exam and was moved to Yard Services in the office. We used to order specialised tools and equipment, anything that was not made in the yard. We started work at eight o'clock, but then we went on to flexi-time. When I went there in 1962 I earned £9 a week, which was good money. (*Mrs Gladys Brushwood, clerical assistant/officer, 1962–79*)

When I first went in in 1972, my weekly wage was £17 and then it gradually increased and I think in 1979 I was getting about £37 a week. Then they brought in flexi-hours and, as long as you did your time, you could build up hours which you could take off as a half day. (*Valerie Willes, clerical assistant, 1972–79*)

Migrant workers: 'only a few of us left now'

The royal dockyards in Britain and overseas were closely linked, and there had always been a degree of mobility, between the dockyards, of

Women were still employed in the Colour Loft until the work was sent out to contractors.

I first went into the dockyard in 1953 because I was a naval widow – my husband was killed in the war. I went in the Colour Loft as a machinist. There were 62 widows working there and I was next to the youngest when I first went in [aged 38]. The old Colour Loft was on the ground floor in a building near to the *Victory*, underneath the Sail Loft.

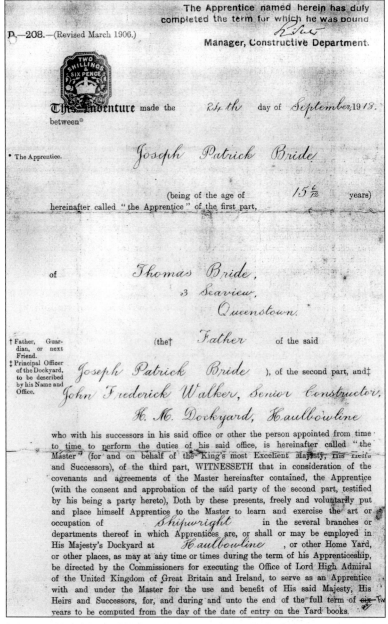

Indentures of Joseph Patrick Bride from HM Dockyard, Haulbowline, Ireland.

dockyards were put on a 'care-and-maintenance' basis and workmen from both these yards came to Portsmouth with their families to make a new life for themselves. Again, in 1950, Bermuda dockyard was closed and 49 apprentices came to Portsmouth dockyard to finish their apprenticeships. The experiences of these migrant workers are varied; some stayed and settled, their children and grandchildren often continuing the tradition of dockyard employment; others came and then left again. There were 39 men, aged around 20, who had started their apprenticeships at Haulbowline.

My husband was an electrical fitter... he worked in the power station in Haulbowline, but went onto ships in Portsmouth. The Irish were not treated well, they were treated like the Blacks are now. When they [the apprentices] got off at the station in Portsmouth, one of them had nowhere to stay and they went to Miss Wallis in Chichester Road. There were three in the same room and they went to the cathedral [St John's Roman Catholic Cathedral] where they had a social club with a billiards room. The also joined St Joseph's Church football team. (*Mrs Rose Lynch, wife of Irish apprentice, 1923*)

I came to England in September 1950 with 48 other Bermudan apprentices. We were excited

personnel and workers. During the 20th century a number of dockyards had to close, either through economy cuts or for political reasons. Such was the case with Haulbowline dockyard in southern Ireland, which was handed over to the Irish Free

State in 1923. All apprentices and established men were given the choice of re-locating to other dockyards, and a number came to Portsmouth in that year. With government cutbacks on defence in the early 1920s, Pembroke and Rosyth

about coming here, as we had heard so much at school about England – the British Empire... It was curious to come and find out, but disappointing when you got here!... we arrived in Portsmouth in the pouring rain. We were put in digs, sometimes four or five of us in one digs. The landlady wanted to know if we could speak English... We felt very upset by our reception... cold rain, stale sandwiches, ignorant people. (*Orien Young, electrical fitter apprentice, 1950–55*)

When we moved to Portsmouth we found out that the neighbours, when they knew it was Pembroke dockyard people coming, they said "Oh, no, not them!"... So many, many Portsmouth people had been put out of work to take the influx of established people in Portsmouth dockyard, its not surprising they were resentful. (*Mrs Kay Barker, child of a skilled labourer, Pembroke dockyard, arrived in 1931*)

There was a lot of Welsh people came down... we had a Pembroke Society [The Pembroke County Club]. We used to have dances and functions... they were very close-knit. They used to have rowing races using naval cutters... the Welsh teams used to battle it out with the Devonians, the Lancashires and the Midlanders, and they used to go from Gosport. The big club was the Caledonian Society, because there were also a lot of Scots in the dockyard. We used to have bowls competitions, tug-of-war... but there's only a few of us left now... the younger ones were born in Portsmouth and they're not interested in Pembroke Dock. (*F.T. Jones, shipwright, 1939–72*)

In 1951, I came to England... I registered at the labour exchange in Lake Road. I came to England because at that time, after the war, the population of Malta was growing and the government requested volunteers to emigrate to Australia, or whatever. I came to Portsmouth because my brother was here... and everyone used to say it was a good place, they used to win the championship [Portsmouth Football Club]! (*Charles Triccas, slinger, 1951–89*)

Getting to work: 'The Dockyard Light Horse'

One of the greatest changes for dockyard employees was

The Unicorn Gate, about 1910.

Dockyard workers
cycling at the
junction of Edinburgh
Road and Fountain
Street, 1950s.

J. LEVY & Cº

FOR
LADIES'
AND
GENT'S
ATTIRE

LEVYS

SWISS CA

RESTAUR

SWISS CAFE

LUNCHEONS | TEAS | DINNER

NAVAL OUTFITTERS   LEVY

TO LET

OODS

in the types of transport that were used to get to and from their place of work. Up until the late 1960s, the favoured mode of transport was the bicycle and many of the people interviewed talked about the hordes of bicycles that left the dockyard gates every midday break, and again in the evenings.

The hooter would go at 12 o'clock and they'd come out in their hundreds... a sea of faces on bikes, no cars, people didn't have cars. My uncle, who lived in Birmingham, when they came down for a holiday, that was the place to be – in Commercial Road to watch the bikes. (*Barbara Chubb, child in Portsmouth during the 1930s*)

This sight was so well known in Portsmouth that it inspired one dockyard worker to write a lengthy poem about the event. The following is a selected extract:

The Dockyard Light Horse
A wonder to many a journalist,
In the days when Britain was
    great,
Was the flood of dockyard
    cyclists
Surging out of the Unicorn Gate.

This highly irregular force
Of cyclists and men was so large,
It was nicknamed the Dockyard
    Light Horse
For it looked like a cavalry
    charge.

Tourists came from miles around
To see this awesome sight
Massed dockyard wheelers
    homeward bound
At noon and also at night.

A dockyard cyclist was able,
Or so old wives would recount,

To reach his dining room table
Without having to dismount.

His wife would open the door
And then stand well to one side
And without his feet touching the
    floor
Straight up the passage he'd ride!
(*J. Clarke 'Nobby the Mobile Poet', shipwright, 1937–82*)

It wasn't really until the 1960s and 70s that people began to drive to the dockyard on motor bikes and in cars, and even then most dockies still used bikes to get to work. (*Bert Lillicrap, shipwright, 1953–95*)

Accidents: 'you're always messing around'

Like most large industrial complexes, the dockyard had its share of accidents and

The steam hammer, HM Dockyard, c.1910.

injuries. However, not all of these were caused by the lack of safety precautions, but some through carelessness or skylarking by workers. A dockyard worker describes one such accident.

He was a driller in the dockyard... we were doing – me and my mate – we were doing a job in the *Victorious's* rudders and he was a driller on the job, and he found a huge great straw sombrero what a sailor had thrown away from abroad... and we went along the dockside, the rudder was laid out, and he was drilling the rivets in it and he was there with this great big sombrero on and it was absolutely hilarious. The only thing that did take the shine off it really was that the bit in the machine bit a bit hard, spun him round and broke his arm, but we still thought he was skylarking 'cos he'd broken his arm and he was holding it up to us and we were calling out "You're a liar, you're always messing around, that's not broken!" – but that's the sort of life it was. (*W.C. Harris, shipwright, 1952–90*)

Such skylarking amongst apprentices was commonplace and as one apprentice engine fitter relates:

They'd stand there talking to you [other apprentices] and at the same time they'd be putting lighted fags in your pocket and the next thing you knew you were on fire! All sorts of jokes like that going on all the time. (*Edward Saunders, engine fitter apprentice, 1941–46*)

They sometimes put a dead rat into a girl's pocket... it was just a bit of teasing! (*Daisy Purvin, armature winder, 1916–19*)

Apprentices were also prone to play tricks on the older men, perhaps to pay them back for the indignities they had to suffer, such as being

HMS *Victory* in dry dock, about 1930.

sent to fetch a 'sky hook' and going for a 'long weight'!

There was an old shipwright, he was one of the old sort who still wore a bowler hat. He used to come in each morning, all dressed up. He had this enormous tool box... he would unlock the box, lift the lid, take off his smart clothes, fold them up and put them in his box, then he would don his overalls and work cap, close the lid and lock his box. A group of shipwright apprentices glued and screwed his box lid down one evening and the next morning they sat and watched while he went through the usual ritual of folding his clothes, but when he went to lift the lid, nothing happened! They were most amused by his bewilderment! (*John Littlefield, shipwright apprentice, 1955–60*)

Safety precautions were one of the main changes in the dockyard, although many aspects of safety were not introduced until the 1960s.

Helmets never came out until quite late... I'm thankful I always wore the helmet when they did come out, 'cos I was on one boat, one of the [aircraft] carriers I think it was, and we were down below on the oil fuel tanks, and the driller had been drilling up the top and his bar and cutter came out of the machine. Me and my pal were standing there talking to the temporary light people... and this thing cracked me across the head... but if it hadn't been for the helmet it would have killed me, there's no

doubt about that, and I was only one with the helmet on, the others were standing there with them in their hands. (*W.C. Harris, shipwright 1952–90*)

I was always impressed, even at that age, by the care which was taken, because we were required to go to the Surgery once a week to get checked over for dermatitis, because we were swilling around in buckets of paraffin... and that was vigorously applied even in those days, long before health and safety acts came into being. Looking back, in most other areas there wasn't any care at all. (*Keith Thomas, electrical fitter apprentice, 1939–44*)

The most frequent one [accident] was the sparking in the eye, but I can remember that the worse one there was from the Joiners' Shop... we had a chappy brought

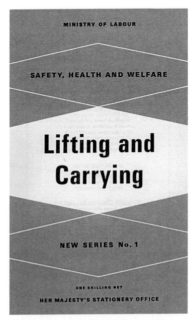

MOD Health & Safety booklet, an edition published in 1968.

in [to the dockyard Surgery] who'd caught his fingers in one of the machines and he lost all his fingers. There were other accidents... there was another terrible accident in one of the machine shops... it was someone getting caught up in the machinery. And I can also remember one... it was very sad... it was when one of the ships was docking and one of the wires broke and whiplashed and killed one of the young sailors on board... that was very sad. But then you had all the mundane things coming in... falling off ladders, things like that. (*Valerie Willes, clerical assistant in dockyard Surgery, 1972–83*)

I went down to the Surgery with Charlie... he'd smacked his thumb with a hammer... we walked in and the doctor had some pincers in his hand, so Charlie said "I don't want to loose my thumb, just lance it". "That's alright" the doctor said, "Follow me", but Charlie was off down the road! (*F.T. Jones, shipwright, 1939–72*)

Facilities in the dockyard: 'you got dirty and you went home dirty'

Another big change in dockyard life was the facilities provided for the employees. Right up until the late 1950s these were extremely primitive, but were largely accepted as part of working life. After World War Two workers were not

'Navy Days', Main Gate, Portsmouth dockyard, about 1960.

prepared to put up with what they saw as inadequate and antiquated facilities. Amenity centres were built around the dockyard in the 1960s.

There were no washing facilities, you got dirty and you went home dirty. There were only box sheds to put your clothes in, so if you got wet, your clothes were still wet when you left. Things did improve greatly after the war and you started getting facilities like changing centres and drying rooms. (*Fred Sampson, boilermaker, 1938–81*)

There were no facilities [for stokers in the Boilerhouse] so

what we used to do unofficially, we used to take a couple of eggs and a bit of bacon and cook it on a shovel... that's true... put it in the fire, get another shovel, shove it full of hot ashes and put the other shovels on top and cook the eggs. (*William Pinch, boilermaker, 1936–83*)

The toilets in the dockyard were dreadful in those days, just open to the elements with long wooden seats and holes cut in over a trough with water running through. It was a favourite trick to wait until a number of dockyardmen had made themselves comfortable and then to light a wad of cleaning cloth,

or a small candle, and float this along the trough under the seats. That always caused great delight for those who did it, but not to the men using the facilities! (*Fred Tucker, shipwright, 1937–82*)

The need for improved facilities was not the only innovation of the post-war period, as increasing concern was shown for the health and safety of workers.

Also you had, which started then, an occupational health side of it which was dealing with getting the men in for screening for this asbestos-type thing, so that they had started it then, screening

Hazard warning.

these people. (*Valerie Willes, clerical assistant in the dockyard Surgery, 1972–93*)

We went for x-rays [checking for asbestosis]... we'd go in a coach to St Mary's Hospital in the first instance, and then they stopped that and they brought the naval x-ray people into the dockyard and we used to go there. If you didn't hear within a fortnight, then okay, you were clear for another year. It's a bit naughty really, because they'd known for years what asbestos could do... there was always asbestos on a ship somewhere. (*W.C. Harris, shipwright, 1952–90*)

I was an insulator in the lagging section and we used to wear nylon navy-blue overalls so that the asbestos from the lagging dust wouldn't stick. We had to change twice a day, we'd change, have a shower, put on new overalls, a new mask and then back on the ships after lunch. We had our own laundry, our own stores to draw the lagging material and we had a separate building with its own amenity room. They came over regularly and tested the level of dust in the

building. We also had full chest x-rays once a year. They were really good on health hazards. (*Tony Rickard, insulator, 1972–94*)

The rundown of the dockyard: 'it will be sadly missed by many'

In 1984 HM Dockyard in Portsmouth was renamed HM Naval Base, and many of the workers point to this date as effectively the end of Portsmouth dockyard. The Falklands War in 1982 had seen the dockyard fully mobilised but, after the fleet returned that year, the decline of Portsmouth dockyard was inevitable. The following years saw the gradual loss of numerous old trades, the merging to two or three trades into one category and the increasing use of technology to replace many of the old skills. The numbers employed dwindled down to a few thousand through early retirement schemes, redundancies and limited recruitment. In 1997 the naval base employed less than 2,000 workers and from April 1998 it has been run by a private company, Fleet Services Ltd.

In June 1981 the defence white paper announced a changed role for the naval base in Portsmouth. We shall still have the same number of ships, but we shall be doing different things to them. We won't do major repairs or modernisation, but we shall be doing straightforward servicing and the work that we previously did here will go to other dockyards (*Captain G.C. Allen RN, Director of the dockyard, 1989*)

When I first went [into the dockyard], there was about 30,000 men, but I would say that progress has changed that... well, you would gradually see less and

Cranes on a building slip, demolished after the construction of HMS *Andromeda* in 1967.

less men. Technology had a lot to do with it... if you rivet a boat up, you might have half a dozen gangs of riveters, about 50-odd men, but when they come in with the welding, they had one man doing it all! (*William Pinch, dilutee shipwright, 1953–58*)

When I left the dockyard it was a different world to the one I had entered... changes from such things as horses and carts or the train to lorries for moving things

The dockyard, including HMS *Victory* and HMS *Warrior* in the heritage area, 1989.

around... the loss of craneage... I remember the shear legs going, they broke and sank when they were being lifted! (*Fred Sampson, boilermaker, 1938–81*)

The mood of the dockyard during these years can perhaps be summed up in an anonymous advertisement that was placed in The Times newspaper by some dockyard workers.

"HM Royal Dockyard Portsmouth passed peacefully away at 12 o'clock last night after nearly 800 years of faithful service. It will be sadly missed by many". (*Advert in The Times, 1 October 1984*)

With all the cutbacks and everything, it wasn't really the same job. It was really getting

very depressing... it was cutbacks on staff – as people were going and they weren't being replaced... they didn't have the resources to do the job properly. I think you were beginning to lose contact with people and having the rapport with them you used to. It just wasn't the same working there. (*Valerie Willes, clerical assistant, 1972–93*)

Conclusions: 'a proud tradition'

This brief overview of Portsmouth dockyard during the 20th century indicates the dominance it has had on the economic and social structures of the town. The history of Portsmouth from the 15th century has been inextricably linked with the Royal Navy and its ships. This

tradition continues to the present day and the dockyard is still a focal point for the townspeople and for visitors. Portsmouth dockyard continues to have a role as a repair and maintenance depot for Britain's navy, and, at the beginning of the 21st century, shipbuilding has returned with the involvement of Vosper Thornycroft. Perhaps more significantly in terms of the relationship between the town and the dockyard, the historic area of the latter has been re-invented as a world-renowned heritage site, one which can proudly present the history of Britain's navy with the presence of three of its most important ships – HMS *Victory*, HMS *Warrior* and the *Mary Rose*.

PORTSMOUTH AT WAR

Stephen Brooks

AS citizens of a dockyard town Portsmouth's inhabitants have always suffered bereavement in wartime, while benefiting from maintaining the navy. In the 20th century these experiences were much more intense. Fatal casualties in World War One were at an extraordinary level, reaching over 5,000 local servicemen. In World War Two the effect of enemy bombing was unique, both in its impact on the population, causing 930 civilian deaths alone, and on the fabric of the city. In the conflicts since, although casualties have been smaller, the anxieties of the relatives of Portsmouth servicemen have perhaps been heightened by better communications.

This chapter largely consists of a selection from one of the richest collections of recordings at the City Museum and Records Office – those concerning Portsmouth and World War Two. The archives hold a wealth of interviews with civilians, including the Home Guard and members of the ARP and other civilian services, and with service personnel from Portsmouth who took part in campaigns overseas, particularly in Normandy. These extracts give a taste of life on the Portsmouth Home Front during six years of 'total war'.

World War One

For centuries Portsmouth's role as the country's leading naval base made it a prime target for enemy attack in time of war. Since the Middle Ages, the Royal Navy and the city's extensive fortifications, heavily armed with guns manned by the garrison, had kept Portsmouth secure. Then in World War One, on 25 September 1916, a German Zeppelin, the L31, raided the city. The airship's bombs are thought to have fallen harmlessly into the harbour, but it was an ominous pointer to the future.

All Portsmouth and Gosport was alight at night with these searchlights. They were all round the hill and the harbour, and they were like a big fan of lights. And this night the bombardment was terrific, so of course Mum woke us up and said, "You'd better go downstairs"... 'Course being kids we waited until she was out one side, then we went and looked out the front door. And as I looked up, looking down the Point, right up that high... it was like a silver cigar... You could see the puffs of the shells they were sending up as they were exploding, and the noise was terrific, but it was too high so it got away... Fantastic. (*Eileen Rayner, born 1905*)

I can remember seeing the Zeppelin, the airship, that come over. We were living in Leonard Road at the time and a policemen

Commemorative plates being distributed to war widows and orphans at a garden fête at Wymering Manor, July 1916.

On the second anniversary of the outbreak of World War One, Portsmouth resolves to fight on.

or somebody come along shouting, "Put the lights out, put the lights out... there's aeroplanes coming!" And our mum gathered us all up in her room, in the front room, and we pushed the chest of drawers up against the door... and then my grandad – 'cos he only took the pub round the corner – he come round shouting up, "Alice, Alice, you alright!" And our mum poked her head out the window. "What you doing out, Dad?" "It's alright", he said, "the airship's gone over". We could see it then in the searchlights... this big silver cigar over the top of us. (*Alfred Woodward, born 1907*)

The casualty list was appalling, especially when Portsmouth-based ships were sunk.

Yes, there was a family next door to us and they had six sons, and four of them were killed within six weeks. Old Portsmouth got very badly hit. Then new people came in. They couldn't stand it. It broke them up, you know. They moved and then there was another woman come there and her husband was in the Navy and – we knew her as Nellie – and her husband was killed. There was quite a lot of them killed from down there. (*Eileen Rayner, born 1905*)

Food shortages led to the introduction of rationing.

The worst thing I remember was the shortage of food, and us having to dash down whenever anyone had margarine in. We used to have to dash off and us

Conductress, 1940. In both world wars women replaced men as conductors on public transport, and in World War Two some became bus drivers.

kids queued up, we queued up for hours. We never had time to get into trouble, we were always hanging around to get food. Then when you got up to the counter, perhaps you'd been two hours in the queue, they'd say "that's the lot, it's all gone!" (*Eileen Rayner*)

World War Two: '...consequently this country is at war with Germany'

Many people very clearly remembered listening to Chamberlain's broadcast on Sunday, 3 September 1939, announcing that the country was again at war with Germany. Some recollected the suffering of World War One, but there was the more immediate expectation that a German bombing campaign would begin within hours. With this in mind plans for the evacuation of the city's children had already been set in motion on 1 September.

I remember the Sunday morning. I was at home in Kingsley Road. I remember exactly where I was standing – in the living room looking at the wireless in the corner and hearing Chamberlain's voice which was rather sepulchral... I was then 20, and a young man, and I remember being horrified at what would immediately happen... There was no doubt in anybody's mind that we would be immediately bombed. (*Sid Wright*)

I think I said to my father, "Will it be like it was when you were in the last war?" He said, "Oh, I expect so". Mother said, "I expect we'll have rationing again. We had rationing in the last war." And that was sort of that. Dad was cross because he was too old... The neighbours came out and said, "Well, it's come to it at last". I just went on with what I was doing. (*Joy Hobbs, dockyard clerk*)

And my father insisted that we all must leave Portsmouth, except my brother who was a Royal Marine, because everyone thought Portsmouth was going to be bombed to the ground on the first day. My two younger brothers, I think, were still away at school, but I went with my mother to relations in Midhurst. It was really quite pleasant. (*Kay Childs, young woman in 1939*)

We got as far as having our bags packed and the labels tied on us and taken to a bus, and at the end of Mafeking Road... at the very last moment my grandmother said, "No!" – I wasn't going, she'd deal with it herself, and we were to come back home. So we got as far as the bus, but never actually got on it. And so that was my experience of evacuation. I didn't go! (*Brian Gray, born 1935*)

We ended up in Ventnor... We were all herded into a hall... and people came in and selected and took them away and in the end there was a sort of nucleus left, of which I was one. As far as I know there were about 12 or 13 boys, and about four girls, and we must have been marched up

Evacuees, 1 September 1939. (By courtesy of *The News*)

to the Burlington Hotel... and more or less dumped on the owner, at least as far as I could see, I don't think she was terribly pleased to have us. And I was there – I was trying to work it out – but I would say about 10-11 months I think. (*Jeanne Niblett, schoolgirl*)

When the German bombing failed to materialise and the period known as the Phoney War began, it provided at least a partial breathing space for people to prepare and to adjust to the facts of wartime life – gas masks, black-out, call-up and rationing.

In the last two years we all really knew there was going to be a war, but we all kept saying, "No there won't, no there won't", and then, when we had it we expected war to start on the Monday... of course, nothing like that happened and life was very much the same. Very peculiar. People walked around wondering what was going to happen and I think that was the big problem: nobody really knew. We had gas masks and suddenly we had rationing... and if you had a light shining you were shouted at, "Put that light out", and life was very much like that for a few months, and then somehow we all got back to things. We went to the cinema again; we went dancing at Kimbell's... (*Geoff Minter, teenager 1939*)

I was sent back to the main battery gun site at Southsea

The staff of Cottage Grove ARP depot, 1939–40.

Common. I went there, it must have been, in October [1939], and when I got there I found there was a great deal of chaos going on because the camp wasn't completed... They were still building huts and so on, and we were all in bell tents, and the weather was atrocious. It rained cats and dogs and the place was full of mud. And we had to camouflage all the tents because they were white and they showed up. (*Gordon Kinch, 214 Battery, 57th Anti-Aircraft Regiment*)

I was in the first call-up once the war had started, and I was the first conscientious objector to register in Portsmouth and this caused a lot of bother at the Labour Exchange in Commercial Road, they just didn't know what to do with me. Where the others were all lined up and rather shouted at... I was treated as I was some superior being, which I found very funny, until they could find the appropriate form for me and know what do with me. (*Stanley Riddell*)

The rationing system was very fair. There was always some who got it on the black market, of course, you'd always get that. But it was fair that everybody got a share... you never went to visit anybody, be it a friend or one of your family, without taking your butter, sugar, tea or milk with you. (*Dorothy Price*)

Mum always said that I did better when I went to the butcher, but it was all under the counter, you

In the mud at the anti-aircraft gun battery on Southsea Common, early in the war.

never saw the kidneys or anything like this, and it was quite possible, if you hadn't been polite to the butcher, that you didn't get offered a sausage or anything like this... but as I say, I did quite well... If you saw a queue you very often went and stood on the end of it in the hopes that what you wanted was at the front. (*Jeanne Niblett, schoolgirl*)

I do remember in the summer, and everything, putting a black pencil line up the back of my legs as if I was wearing stockings... by the time I got to 17 we were a bit conscious of things we were going without, but of course to have stockings with a seam... was the thing, so we used to just draw pencil marks. (*Sheila Duce*)

We could get parachutes – you could buy them. I think they were about 5s and they were beautiful silk – this lovely off-white silk – great panels. They must have had a surplus of them in this country and they were selling them off. And you can imagine, you know, the size of the parachute and all those big panels were this beautiful soft silk, and we used to make our underwear and blouses with them and I've heard ladies say they made their trousseaus with them. (*Joyce Cross, teenager*)

Smitten city

The bombing of Portsmouth finally started on 11 July 1940 with a daylight raid which resulted in 18 deaths.

Daylight raids could seem very personal:

The first air raid on Portsmouth in July 1940 came at the end of a day when the siren had been going all through the day. We continually went to the air raid shelter, but nothing happened until late afternoon when again the siren went and caught us unawares. The German bombing began almost instantaneously and while I was sauntering – I hadn't realised anything was going to happen – sauntering across to the air raid shelter, a German fighter plane appeared from nowhere and dived down in front of me and machine-gunned me as walked across the [barracks] square. I could see the German pilot with his goggles on and the machine gun fired. I was just paralysed, rooted to the spot... It frightened the life out of me. I couldn't work properly and the junior commander took me to the MO, who said I should have a week's leave which I did, recovered, and I got used to the air raids after that. (*Nancy Jackson, serving in the ATS*)

Now that the bombing had begun the people of Portsmouth had to try to adjust to nights in the air raid shelters which had long been awaiting this eventuality. Some preferred to take their chances under the stairs, while others went 'over the hill' and joined the nightly trek out of the city. In early 1942 – after the worst of the bombing was over – complex tunnel shelters in Portsdown Hill provided another refuge.

I was living with [my husband] Jack's mother by now, so I went into her air-raid shelter and there was her and her elderly lodger... the whole time we were in that air-raid shelter this elderly lady used to pray. She prayed all night long, all the hours we were in that air-raid shelter she sat there with her hands together praying out loud. Anyway we spent several hours down there and

Doris Bealing's cousins and a friend on a smallholding at Cowplain, July 1941, where they had been sent away from the bombing.

after a raid I was always sick. (*Dorothy Price*)

We had a brick air raid shelter put in. I think we spent one night in it and it was terrible, everything was loud, the vibration of any bombs falling was exaggerated in these, and we didn't feel a bit safe. We just felt that the concrete roof was going to fall on us and we felt a lot safer indoors under the stairs. (*Margaret Herridge, schoolgirl, Stamshaw*)

We used to go to Clanfield. And my next-door neighbour – he worked for a big firm in Portsmouth that had a big van – so him and his family what weren't evacuated, and Jill and I, she being the youngest... we use to go out to Clanfield every night and come in in the morning, so we done that for quite a long time. (*Elsie Keld, born 1897*)

When we arrived at the tunnels... we'd dash round to see the fan starting up for the fresh air, and it was a huge thing as big as this room... I can also remember the fact that the men used to hang their alarm clocks on the corners of their bunk beds for getting up in the morning. I think they probably worked in the dockyard... I don't think we had a great deal of contact with people. You just went there to have a good night's sleep and a bit of peace and quiet, away from the bombing. (*Sheila Justice, child*)

It is recorded that there were 67 bombing raids on Portsmouth. At the end of a raid those who escaped with their lives might nevertheless find that they had lost family and friends; homes, possessions, livelihoods; physical and mental well-being.

... I said to Curly, had he got the tea ready? I was just having a cup of tea and talking to my friend John Wareham and that is all I know – Johnny Wareham got killed, the two men behind the bar got killed and I believe we had a messenger with us, I am not sure about that but I believe we did – anyway he got killed and there was only three of us

Bomb damage at Conway Street School, near Unicorn Gate, December 1940.

Looking across Southsea to St Paul's Church, bombsites mostly from the raid of 10 January 1941.

got out. Two of us were injured – and that is all I remember about that because as I said, I was unconscious from then on... My helmet was still on my head at the time, and when I did finally come away from the hospital, they asked me, do you want to take your helmet with you? Well, when I looked at this helmet it had four big dents in it that I could put my fingers in but no real holes. (*Fireman Gordon Emery, injured when his station in Madden's Hotel was bombed on 27 April 1941; 28 others were killed.*)

I worked in the homeless centres... We were called in every time there was a bombing raid. I

think the worst one was just before Christmas [1940] when the outside of the dockyard was flattened, all around Unicorn Gate... When they came out they were in their night-clothes, perhaps a coat and slippers, and that was all they had. They were brought up to the homeless centres and that particular night Lady Daley, who was the Lady Mayoress, had got a clothing stall where she had collected up all the clothes, and she came in and opened that clothing stall up so people could have some clothes. (*Joy Hobbs, dockyard clerk*)

What I found frightening was the fires... I was working at Portsmouth dockyard when

King's Road and Elm Grove were fire bombed... I had to get to work so I was walking... I met one of the girls from the office and I said to her, "I can't walk down there!" "Yes you can", she said and she grabbed my arm and we walked down through these burnt-out shells, but it was quite terrifying. (*Dorothy Price*)

January the 10th... Everywhere in Portsmouth was burnt out and burning... A busy night, and my friends who owned ponies, i.e. greengrocers' ponies, we went to find out if we could do anything for the ponies and they were all gone! So we spent the best part of the night searching Portsmouth to find them, and about dawn next day we discovered a whole rodeo of assorted ponies and horses that had been cooped up in the United Services ground... There were bakers' horses, the coalman's, Pickfords' horses. Anybody that had horses, had horses in that football ground. (*Pat Pope, teenager*)

Geoff Minter was due to start work at Lloyds Bank in Commercial Road on the morning of 11 January 1941:

I went there that day and that was the day after the bad bombing in Commercial Road, and there was no Lloyds Bank; it was just flat. I said to the policeman, "I start work here today", and he said, "They won't need you today". So I went in and said, well, I must see someone. I saw the manager and said, "My name is Minter, sir. I start today." He said, "Well, don't stand there, get a spade and start digging. We've got the FA Cup under here and an IOU from Lord Nelson for half-a-crown, so get digging!" So that was my first job in the bank. (*Geoff Minter, teenager*)

The destruction of the Guildhall during the blitz of 10/11 January 1941 was a symbolic blow to the city. Ken Hampton of the City Police Fire Brigade was on the spot:

It suddenly dawned on us that it was possible that one of these incendiaries had found its way into one of the ventilators, of

Paratroopers helping clear rubble in Silver Street, Southsea.

which there were several up on the roof... And, of course, when we opened up one of them we saw then that one of the incendiaries had gone down through the slots and finished up at the bottom of the ventilator and it was well alight... We came down floor by floor, with the fire coming down after us. We had no means of stopping it – no water. When we got down to the main hall, and this is something I won't forget, we saw the whole of the ceiling all a big red glow where it was burning through and of course lumps were dropping off on to the main floor of the hall, which of course immediately set it alight. (*Ken Hampton*)

I walked up towards the Guildhall. Well, you didn't need a torch. It was just red and orange.

The whole city was lit. It was like daylight, and I just walked up to it... The ARP men and the police and the firemen had a fit when they saw me coming along. I was in uniform and so they accepted that. And there were all the pipes and you had to step over them all because they were doing nothing, they couldn't, they just didn't have any water... The Guildhall had already lost its top and the shell was just an inferno. It was horrific, red, orange, yellow flames leaping out. And what was coming out was floating down in the air, like very big snowflakes. (*Cynthia Bartlett*)

... Portsmouth born man, a Portsmouth family man,[it was] the end of the world, to see the Guildhall going. You knew there was no hope, it was going to go. Never thought the outside part

Albert S. White, photographed in 1939 or 1940.

Aid Parties Depot at Kent Road. A time-bomb exploded, trapping people under the debris:

We just set about to make sufficient of a hole in the wall to get the people out... We thought there were five people, but I couldn't see them... We went ahead and I could see this chap was a bit dodgy and he was going to move and have the whole lot down if we weren't careful. So I sent Bill Lane over to see the sister in charge of the First-Aid Post and told her what problem we had and she said, "I'll keep him quiet for you". So she came over and evidently gave him some morphine or something... We managed to get him on the stretcher blanket to get him away. Meanwhile our other colleague, who was on the outside, Betty Fortune, she said, "This chimney isn't going to last any heavy bombing"... I said, "How bad?" And she said, "It is moving". And I nodded to the others and said, "What shall we do about it?" And we said, "Well, let's get them out". And we stayed and got them out. (*Albert White*)

Albert White was awarded the George Medal, as were Bill Lane and Len Wilson, who assisted him in the rescue.

would stand up like it did. I thought next time I saw it it would have been collapsed in... The Guildhall was important to us, you know. (*Harold Ellis, born 1902*)

Countless individual acts of bravery were performed during the bombing raids on Portsmouth. Two which were recognised by the award of the George Medal took place on the night of the second major blitz on the city on 10/11 March 1941. Albert White was the Assistant Superintendent of the First-

That same night in Southsea PC Goronwy Evans found himself directed to a blitzed house on the corner of Elm Grove and St Andrew's Road. The house was alight and

there was a nursing home next door.

Well, you had the bombs dropping and you were a little bit apprehensive, because the place was an absolute shambles. Anyway, I got in through a window, clambered over all the stuff and got this bucket of water, and then a chain of buckets of water, working with this stirrup pump. Well, apparently, I must have been overcome by fumes a couple of times, and one of the other policemen got me out, and then I was back in. Anyhow, we managed to put it out eventually, and made certain it was alright. (*Goronwy Evans*)

It fell to the Assistant Chief Constable to inform PC Evans that he had been awarded the George Medal:

He went to great lengths to say that the honour was not just for

PC Goronwy Evans, wearing his George Medal.

me, but the honour of the force, in other words, you know, "You only did what any other policeman would have done". (*Goronwy Evans*)

In the bombing of Portsmouth, 930 civilians and many service personnel were killed, and 1,216 civilians seriously injured. After each raid there was the 'clearing up' to do – a bit of excitement for youthful collectors of shrapnel, a grim and haunting experience for the men of the city's Central Depot:

After a raid it was always good for the next morning to go to school – I went to Trent Road School – hunt for shrapnel and go home with pockets full. I used to have quite a collection in the war, and my trophy was on top of the shelter. It was quite a mound. (*Brian Gray, schoolboy*)

We in Central Depot... operated the dead body recovery scheme... We would be saddled with the responsibility of picking up the corpses off the street. A very shattering experience... I and one or two others would find

John Dean and other volunteer ARP messengers.

ourselves driving refuse vehicles to pick up the corpses... (*Frank Deacon*)

Separation and loss

The following extracts provide a glimpse of the suffering and sadness experienced by Portsmouth people parted temporarily or permanently from their loved ones. Yet those interviewed talk of high morale, enhanced community spirit and even cheerfulness in the face of such adversity, something which is, by and large, supported by contemporary sources.

[My father] was at one time on HMS *Hood*, which was sunk afterwards, but then he went on to the *Royal Oak*, which was torpedoed in October [1939] in Scapa Flow. I remember going down to the barracks with my mother and there was a loudspeaker high up on the wall and we were waiting for the names of survivors to come through. With my friend we went up and down the street, touching all the wooden windowsills, and saying, "Touch wood my daddy isn't dead". Those are my most vivid memories, and I can remember my aunts being there and my mother crying, but they kept a lot of the sorrow from us as children. (*Doris Bealing, primary schoolgirl*)

Sunday morning I had this casualty telegram to deliver, and I was only, what, 15 years of age,

and I went to the door, knocked, the door was answered and, of course, as soon as I opened it, she just literally broke down and sobbed her heart out... I can always recall knocking the next-door neighbour's house, and asking if she would come in and be with her while I continued on my delivery of telegrams... I can remember one instance in Portsea after one of the major raids. I went down there, and the firemen were still fighting the blazes and seeing a wall come down as they were fighting it, but that was not as traumatic as delivering a casualty telegram... I can recall when HMS *Hood* went down, being a Portsmouth-based ship, I had 60 telegrams, all casualty telegrams, to deliver in the North End area. (*Norman Cross, teenager*)

As soon as I took the telegram – I was at my mother's that day – they had gone out to visit my brother's wife and I took the telegram, I didn't have to open it because we had a code: if he had to send a telegram it would be to my 'pet' name, which no one else knew about. But as soon as I saw it was addressed to me formally, I didn't have to open it. It was the usual one, "The Admiralty regret to inform you" – it's all you get. (*Joy Hobbs, widowed in 1944*)

[My father] didn't come home in the morning, and I said to Mum, "Where's dad?" as we come out of the air-raid shelter... and I went to school and when I was at school one of the boys said to me, "I hear your father's got killed", and I said, "No, he's

Ivor Fairbrother and his father Tom, a member of a rescue squad killed in 1941.

alright"... It wasn't till I got back from school in the evening, to see my sister, that she told me that my father had been killed... That really broke my heart... 'cos I loved my father. (*12-year-old Ivor Fairbrother, whose father was in an ARP squad*)

My father was never a well man and when I went away abroad he started getting heart trouble, and when I did get a letter in Burma it was generally telling me my father was dying. There was nothing you could do. Nowadays they would probably say 'compassionate leave', but you were in Burma and he was home here... He died soon after I got home... I had a nervous breakdown and in those days there was no counselling. Out of desperation I went up to Locksway Road to the mental home up there and they told me to clear off. They said, you're just

The king and queen visit Portsmouth, 1941. On the left is Sir Denis Daley, lord mayor. (By courtesy of *The News*)

a worrier. I used to wander the streets. It was the conditions I'd been under and I couldn't do anything about it. I'm sure to this day [it was] just worrying what my mother would do if my father had died and me and brother out there. (*Burma campaign veteran*)

The Second Front

In 1944 the Portsmouth harbour area would be the nerve centre for the launch of the Allied invasion of Normandy, but the disastrous raid on Dieppe in August 1942 had shown how much needed to be done to ensure success.

I was going home from work that day and I was walking to towards the main gate when all these

Canadian troops came marching up from South Railway Jetty and they really looked as if they had been in a scrap. The next thing we knew there were air raid sirens and gunfire going off. The Germans had obviously followed the remnants of the troops back from Dieppe to Portsmouth and were trying to find them. There was a heavy fog at the time that sort of saved the day. But those poor troops really looked as if they had been through hell and back. (*Adrian Taylor, born 1923, dockyard apprentice*)

Hundreds of thousands of American troops were transported to Britain to take part in the invasion of Normandy and this 'friendly invasion' brought some much-appreciated glamour to wartime Portsmouth.

I just remember them in uniform coming down the road and the girls they were going out with looking as proud as punch that they were going out with an American, you know? And Americans had money to flash around and nylons and things like that, and some of the kids running over, "You got any gum, chum?" (*Margaret Herridge, schoolgirl*)

By the spring of 1944 preparations for Operation Overlord, as the Normandy invasion was known, were taking place in every part of Portsmouth as the forces gathered. One mysterious aspect of these preparations was the construction of units of the artificial Mulberry harbours – massive concrete blocks for the breakwaters

A direct hit on the Airspeed administration block, 1941.

and smaller concrete 'beetles' to support the floating roadways.

...there was a lot more wooded areas around Portsmouth at the time, and in amongst the trees were all these camps with tanks and various military vehicles hidden amongst the trees... Mum had three Welshmen billeted on her. We were in Francis Avenue then and they were working at Hayling Island on this project. They were absolutely in the dark, although they were working on the project, and they said, "We're making these boats, but we're making them out of concrete, and they sink" (*Jeanne Niblett, schoolgirl*)

We had to report to the Labour Exchange, and they sent us out to Southsea – out to Clarence Pier – where we had to build 'beetles'. Mind you, it was hard work, but what made you work harder was the cold. The wind coming of the sea was bitter, but we got so warm working that we could take off our overcoats, but once you stopped you quickly froze, but we were pouring in the concrete, and doing the steel just the same. We had no idea what we were building... There was barbed wire everywhere, and there was a bloke who stood with a machine gun at the entrance to Clarence Pier so nobody could come in and have a look round,

but anyway, there was nothing to see except concrete. (*Reg Pinwill*)

Secrecy was maintained to the very end, but the possibility of a surprise attack on Portsmouth to disrupt Overlord was taken seriously.

It was building up to D-Day and I think they suspected that there might be a paratroop attack on our communications... I had a rifle and a sten gun, and during the guard duty of Telephone House, we were guarding the relay room, I think in the basement, and I was told, quite seriously, to shoot anybody who came through that door. When I said, well, how about if it's one of ours, the order was to shoot him, whoever it is, shoot him. I just could not believe that the order was given. (*George Mason of the 17th (Portsmouth) Battalion of the Hampshire Home Guard*)

We were aware that something was on, but whether it was going to be a huge exercise, or the invasion, we didn't know. I got my instructions to be out on the common in the vicinity of Ladies' Mile about four o'clock in the morning... We were posted about 50 yards apart to form a sort of alley... and the next thing we knew some time after four o'clock the troops arrived,

marching, all ready to go... and our instructions were that no-one was to get anywhere near them and neither were they to get in touch with anybody in any shape or form, and that's what we did... (*Detective Constable Joseph Watson*)

D-Day was delayed for 24 hours by the weather, but then the Supreme Commander, General Eisenhower, gave the word to go at his Southwick House headquarters just outside Portsmouth.

On the day before D-Day, when they had just made their decision, we had been to get our pay,

which was 15s and a soap coupon, and we were walking back when I heard the guard come to attention, and I said, "Something's happening. Let's wait a minute." And out of the door came Eisenhower and Ramsay and Tedder and Leigh-Mallory, and they saw us gaping up at them, and Eisenhower gave us the thumbs-up sign and we knew it was on. (*Wren Jeanne Law, on duty at Southwick House*)

On the night that the fleet sailed, the number of planes going over was absolutely colossal. It even woke us up, and that took some doing because we were so dead-beat; and then in the morning we

Soldiers preparing to embark from South Parade Pier, shortly after D-Day.

looked out into the harbour and it was empty, and there had been anything upwards of 5,000 ships out there – you could have walked across them out to Spithead practically. (*Olive Pearce, Wren*)

In the aftermath of D-Day, casualties and German prisoners-of-war had to be dealt with as they arrived in Portsmouth; women, as in so many aspects of the war effort, played a major role.

... it was wave after wave, and some of the boys were clean, some of them had been laying in mud, some obviously hadn't had

a wash... One chap who was badly burned said to me, "I'm quite good-looking really you know nurse". I said, "Your eyes are not bad now, they're quite saucy". So he said, "You wouldn't like to give us a kiss, would you, nurse?" We weren't allowed, but I looked around and I bent down and kissed him on his horribly burnt lips with the awful smell coming up from his burns. (*Mary Verrier, member of a Red Cross Voluntary Aid Detachment at St Mary's Hospital, Portsmouth*)

You'd suddenly be called on because there was a landing craft coming in at South Railway Jetty. It would be some German

prisoners-of-war, or some wounded and could you go down and help and either escort the prisoners or act as stretcher-bearers. The Germans were badly shaken. They didn't say much. Having lost several friends I sort of hated them at the time, but when you saw how they were reacting you felt sorry for them. (*John Rogers, Dockyard Home Guard, born 1927*)

As the Allies struggled to achieve their break-out from Normandy, Hitler bombarded southern England with the first of his 'revenge weapons' – the V1 flying bomb. Fortunately only two struck

Rescue and clearance after the flying bomb at Stamshaw, 1944.

Victory in Europe Day party, Aylesbury Road, Buckland.

Portsmouth. The second of these hit Newcomen Road, Stamshaw on 15 July 1944 and resulted in 15 deaths.

The flying bomb... landed at the end of the next street and all the houses at the end were flattened... we lost all the windows in our house, except in the kitchen. We were trying to get to our own shelter and we had just got as far as the kitchen, and I think that window escaped because there was a high wall opposite which stopped the blast. But I can remember the glass and the debris falling for quite a long time and we just stood there and screamed. (*Doris Bealing, schoolgirl*)

Peace returns

Hostilities in Europe officially ended on 8 May 1945 – VE-Day – and the city rejoiced, with ships' sirens sounding, street parties, bonfires and a Service of Thanksgiving in Guildhall Square.

When it happened everybody seemed to be ready. All sorts of things appeared. The flags, the Union Jacks and the extra bits of food, and fireworks. And I can remember that night, all along the Stamshaw foreshore, there was a big bonfire at the bottom of every street, because we just walked along and everyone was so happy... On the actual day of VE-Day we went out on a bus and we went through the Guildhall Square and it was absolutely full of people and I just remember rings of people dancing. I think I can remember some French sailors. They were the ones who had the red pom-poms on their hats. Then we got to Southsea and it was absolutely packed... all along the promenade. My aunt picked a red, white and blue flower to make a buttonhole. She got told off by a policeman, but he had a twinkle in his eye, he wasn't really cross... (*Doris Bealing*)

When I got to the Guildhall Square I stood and watched a sailor climb right up the flagstaff and he threw all his clothes away! Two sailors were standing at the bottom of the Guildhall steps, with a crowd of women cheering them on, doing a striptease dance until they had thrown all their clothes away. (*Stanley Riddell, born 1917*)

Everyone had a party. In fact, everybody used to gatecrash. The pubs were full up at Eastney... We went in all of them, didn't we? And we all had a drink, and it was lovely because people were so different. Someone would bring a piano out, and from each bedroom window there would be all the bunting and the flags... and, of course, we had all made jellies and sandwiches and what the ration would allow, and long tables were laid out in the middle of the road and it went on for days... (*Pat Lake, worker at Airspeed*)

The surrender of Japan in August 1945 finally brought the war to an end. Happiness and relief were mixed with sadness over those who had not lived to see the return of peace and uncertainty about the future.

The relief was wonderful, but I didn't like bangers and everything anymore, the flashing, and although it was fireworks and not guns flashing, I didn't like it. (*Sheila Duce, born 1926*)

Elise and Doris Waters – alias Gert and Daisy – sisters and performers in variety, visiting the NAAFI in Alexandra (now Museum) Road, late in the war.

There was no real celebration in our part of the world [Hayling Island]. It was just relief that we could think about the future. Not that we knew how to, because we were all in a pretty bad shape, really. We'd lived on our nerves, just going along with it all... So at the end of the war we were all a bit confused, I suppose, and tired and didn't quite know what we were meant to do next... It was all a bit flat, I thought. (*Nancy Jackson*)

The war had ended and everyone was jolly happy, but on the other hand there was more tears shed then than at any other time. People had talked about people killed and missing, and not coming back, and all this sort of thing, but there wasn't a lot of tears shed then, but at the end of the war there was an awful lot of crying went on. And I thought, as a youngster, this was a most peculiar thing. (*Brian Gray, schoolboy*)

Postscript

Although this chapter has focused on the 1939-45 period, war has continued to have an impact in many ways on the lives of the people of Portsmouth, most notably at the time of the Falklands Conflict in 1982. The following extracts have been chosen to represent some reactions to it.

We had the news on, the boys had just gone to bed, and it just come on, it said HMS *Sheffield* had been hit and the neighbours

HMS *Hermes* leaving Portsmouth for the Falklands, 5 April 1982.

all came round, crying and that. I tried to phone up and some chap said that I'd have to wait a couple of days before I'd actually know what had happened to him... I had to wait until half-past six the next morning before a chaplain phoned up to say that he was still alive. (*Margaret Bailey, whose husband was serving in HMS* Sheffield *during the Falklands Conflict*)

I can remember the sky going grey the day the *Coventry* was hit. I happened to be in the Portsmouth Harbour area and it was a really sad and gloomy day and the whole mood of the people was downcast. (*Denise Daly, serving as a Wren in Portsmouth when her husband's ship, RFA* Tidespring, *was sent to the Falklands in 1982*)

Mrs Daly stopped watching the nine o'clock news:

There was never any advanced warning of anything that happened at all. Invariably, if it was bad news, it came on the nine o'clock news because of the time lapse between the Falkland Islands and here, and that's really why I changed my routine. I felt that in the cold light of morning, if I got into the office and learned of something that had happened, I could deal with it much better in the daylight. (*Denise Daly*)

At the end of the conflict, ships of the Task Force were welcomed back to Portsmouth:

People were just happy to have their loved ones home and if that meant throwing up some coloured smoke and some noise, boats in the harbour escorting the ships home, fine, but I think people's reaction was more of relieved than anything, that it was all finished. (*Denise Daly*)

LEISURE, PLEASURE AND ENTERTAINMENT

Eva Balogh

LEISURE, for most people, means doing something both pleasurable and relaxing and, perhaps most importantly, time away from the working environment. It is essential to remember that 'work' relates not just to paid employment. Unpaid work, such as childcare or housework, also requires a respite. Equally, for children, leisure may mean not being at school or an 'escape' from the family. Twentieth-century Portsmouth, as a seaside holiday resort and an important naval base, offered its inhabitants and visitors a wide range of choice of leisure pursuit. An individual's own interpretation of 'leisure', is dependent on a variety of factors, among them: class, gender, race and age. Those factors have also changed over time.

It is impossible to cover, in this short chapter, all aspects of leisure in the city, or all perspectives on it, but hopefully, most of the more popular pursuits are included. It is hoped, also, that the reader will gain some real insight into the experience of leisure, pleasure and entertainment in the City of Portsmouth as it changed and developed throughout the 20th century.

Sitting in the back row...

The Victoria Hall (1855-1959) in Commercial Road can

A cup-tie crowd at Fratton Park, 1 Feb 1908.

The Plaza cinema, 1930s, the first cinema in Portsmouth to show 'talkies'.

boast of being the first theatre in Portsmouth to show 'moving pictures', in 1896. Since that date, the cinemas of Portsmouth have played host to thousands of films, providing a source of entertainment and pleasure for millions of people, although not solely from the films on offer, because the cinema has also been a place for lovers to meet, for children to immerse themselves in to a world of fantastic adventure and also, a place where life-long relationships were formed.

The cinemas of Portsmouth have experienced enormous popularity (there were 24

purpose-built cinemas in the city by 1937), a serious decline during the 1960s and 1970s and, during the last decade, welcome evidence of revival with the arrival of the UCI at Port Solent and the Warner multiplex at Gunwharf.

As a child I went to the Globe cinema near St Mary's church... I can remember paying a penny to go there... There was Lillian Gish and her sister, Charlie Chaplin, Laurel & Hardy. Some of the films were horrific and frightened me to death! When the woman was on the train line and the train was coming, and she was going to be cut up into pieces! (*Betty Sayers, 1920s*)

This experience may seem rather extraordinary if compared to modern films but as the following memory reveals, the effect of films on children was a major concern.

I helped to show *Snow White and the Seven Dwarfs* the first time it was shown in Portsmouth... first to the managers and their wives and the Watch Committee, because they were deciding, on that Thursday morning, to make it a universal (U) or an adult (A) because of the scenes in the wood where they run through the woods screaming. (*Arthur Limburn, cinema projectionist, 1930s*)

However, by the 1950s, children had become accustomed to the thrill and excitement of the cinema and children's cinema clubs flourished.

The first thing they did before the start of the programme was the manager, who I can only remember as Uncle John who was a dapper chap – he had a pinstripe suit and a moustache – would stand on the stage and try to get these kids – about 500 kids – to be quiet whilst he made various announcements... He also introduced a sing-song and the words came up on the screen... I can only remember the first few words, "We come along on a Saturday morning and greet everybody with a smile"... Some would sing it, when they weren't fighting with the kid next to them! (*Terry Butler, 1950s*)

We used to go to the Gaumont picture club for children... on Saturday morning. It was great fun, I mean, it was a great sense of camaraderie to be in a cinema full of nothing but children under the age of 12, and no parents around. And we used to really get in the spirit of the films and cheer in the right places and boo in the right places... There was a club song that used to be sung with great relish. The last line used to disappear because as the last line was being sung the curtains would open and the main morning film would come up and the last remaining words used to disappear into a big cheer! (*David Reeves, 1950s*)

However, although the children certainly had a great time, the staff had a totally different experience!

Terribly noisy! We used to keep flashing our lights telling them to shut up, but it didn't make any difference! They used to ride the back of the seats as cowboys... and throw things at one another. It used to be murder!... but the kids enjoyed it. (*Betty Weston, usherette at The Regent cinema, North End, 1940s*)

For some children, actually getting in to the cinema was an adventure in itself.

There used to be a picture house called The Old Vic and you'd 'bunk in' there. One would go in, maybe one would pay... when the lights came up in the interval you had to duck down under the seats so they couldn't see who was in and who wasn't... The old

Palace Cinema was quite unusual because the cinema was right behind the door, so you went in, and instead of seeing the screen in front of you, you actually had to turn round. It was very difficult to 'bunk in' at The Palace because there was only one door you could open and because it was so small you stood every likelihood of getting seen. I can remember 'bunking in' once with a couple of cousins and when the lights came up there were only four people in the place, and they obviously knew because we got hooked out and it was always slightly shamefaced being thrown out on to Commercial Road in those days. (*Michael Hancock, young cinema attendee, 1950s*)

Of course, the cinema was not just a place for children to indulge in fantasy and adventure. The film stars themselves, particularly from

Cinenews showed only newsreels. Within a year of its opening in 1936 it had become a conventional cinema.

A starlet visiting the Carlton Cinema, Cosham, 1955, photographed by Ken Pratt.

the 1930s projected a world of glamour that appealed to many.

I used to get lost in a lot of those films and I used to do my hair the way the film stars did theirs. I would have loved to have been a film star. That – working as an usherette – was the nearest I could get to it! (*Florence Wall, usherette at The Ambassador Cinema, Cosham, The Carlton Cinema, Cosham, and The Plaza Cinema, Bradford Junction, 1940s*)

Greta Garbo was our favourite... my friend and I used to just love Greta Garbo. We went to see her

first talking film at The Regent at North End. It was a lovely place, nice foyer to it and really beautiful. (*Vera Roberts, 1930s*)

For others, perhaps it was neither the film nor the stars that was the main attraction!

I always tried to sit in the back row so no-one could see we were cuddling each other... make for the back row in those days because it was the only quiet place you could go for a little cuddle. (*Jack Price, 1930s*)

At The Plaza, if you went as a young couple, like we did on a couple of occasions, if you paid

2s 3d [11p] you could go right at the back and they had double seats where you could have a cuddle! (*David and Ann Hayward, 1950s–'60s*)

The staff could also experience pleasure from the cinema for a number of reasons.

You used to get lots of dates... fellas used to [laughing] you know!... of course we were all nice and clean and smart. (*Vera Ayres, usherette at The Ambassador Cinema, Cosham, 1940s*)

We had green [uniforms], we had

The city's volunteer lifeguard corps has been saving the lives of unwary bathers since the 1920s. (By courtesy of *The News*)

orange reveres and a kick pleat on each knee, where orange kicked out. A little green hat with orange round it, like a pillbox... we had a wide cuff, done in orange, with the gold braid on the cuff. Oh they were very smart, really. (*Betty Weston, usherette at the Tivoli cinema, Copnor, 1940s*)

Although, on occasions, the usherettes had more than just the 'noisy kids' to contend with!

They [the projectionists], used to put a spotlight on you... I used to have an argument with the projectionist because he would keep the spotlight on 'em... he used to do it on purpose! (*Molly Rowe, usherette at The Regent Cinema, North End, 1933–78*)

The sailors... weren't the most polite people... they used to look at you as part of the entertainment... we had to stand our ground with some of them! (*Eva Hunt, usherette at The Shaftesbury Cinema, Kingston Road, 1940s–'50s*)

There were queues and queues and queues every weekend and Sundays... in the interval, when the lights were up, we had to stand on the line – what we called standing on the line – and that was to stop the people in the cheaper seats jumping back to the dearer seats! Of course, all the 'Cosham Boys', they knew I was a shy person and they used to make remarks, you know, and tease me and my face used to be beetroot red! (*Florence Wall, usherette at The Ambassador Cinema, Cosham, 1940s*)

The transformation of the Cinema during the 1990s has ensured its survival in the

ever-competitive arena of the leisure industry, although going to the cinema nowadays is undoubtedly a completely different experience to that of the past.

I still go to the pictures, probably on a weekly basis. Mainly the ones in town – the Odeon and the ABC. I sometimes go over to the UCI at Port Solent if someone's taking me but, because I have no transport, it's not very accessible... I tend to like 'odd' films rather than mainstream... or if they have certain people in or directors. I'll go just because they are in it... I don't find cinemas as full as when I was younger. Most of the time they're not full and they're a lot smaller now because they've got three or four screens... and now, they turf you out at the end of the film whereas before you could stay in there all day! (*Jackie Bryden, 1998*)

But, the cinema still has other attractions to offer, apart from the film...

If we've all got some money, we might go to the cinema... Cosham or Portsmouth... If we're going to the cinema, then we'll get dressed up 'cos we'll go and try to pull boys! (*Layla Garner, 15-year-old cinema viewer, 1998*)

Limelight

An alternative to the cinema was the theatre, professional or amateur. Portsmouth had six theatres and music halls

The Portsmouth Players in an unidentified production of the 1950s.

in 1901; most fell victim to competition from cinema and, later, television.

Oh yes, yes the Coliseum was a favourite for my mother, that was in Edinburgh Road... and I often used to go with my mum, and sometimes a neighbour, when we lived in Locksway Road. I remember a neighbour coming with us on one occasion... We saw a pantomime, Dad and I, at the Theatre Royal and I have never heard of it or seen it since and it was called *Goodie Two Shoes*. And I remember the name of it, but it was obviously a ballerina I would think – something about a ballerina – and my dad took me. Then there was the Hippodrome [opposite the Theatre Royal]. Of course that was bombed. We used to go to the Hippodrome a lot, and my husband and I went when we first knew one other. I've seen

Evelyn Laye at the Hippodrome, we've seen Jack Warner's sisters, Elsie and Doris Waters – the comedians – we have seen them at the Hippodrome. We had all the stars come to the theatres... (*Vera Cole, remembering the 1910s–'30s*)

Well, my dad worked in the Hippodrome... He would get complimentary tickets and we would go to the special shows, and always to the pantomime. That was free, you see? Take your oranges with you... I can remember the smell now. Everybody at the pantomime seemed to have oranges and they would be peeling them, and my mother would take a loaf of bread and she would put it between her knees and cut these slices of bread and put the margarine on and a sprinkle of sugar. I think this was tea, oranges and tea and she would

Southsea beach, 1984.

pass it all along the row... We always got there free. We couldn't have gone otherwise. (*Gladys Fisher, young in the 1920s–'30s*)

They took me to the Theatre Royal to see *The Maid of the Mountains* and that was an original production there then. That really started me off on my love of musical shows. I have seen a good many musical shows... but all that came into our parties, whatever was the latest. *Maid of the Mountains* and *The Desert Song*. (*Joy Hobbs, 1920s–'30s*)

'Oh, I do like to be beside the seaside!'

One of the main attractions of Portsmouth has always been Southsea and its seafront. Since the Victorian

era it has been marketed and developed. 'Come to Sunny Southsea' was an enticing slogan and, with its promenade, piers, funfair and common, Southsea has been a place of entertainment for both local people and holidaymakers. However, as with many British seaside resorts, Southsea has, more recently perhaps, lost some of its appeal. A huge growth in the foreign travel market has undoubtedly contributed to this decline; to compensate the city has invested in Portsmouth's naval heritage. But, for many, the beach, on a hot summer day or a balmy evening, still remains one of the biggest attractions that Portsmouth can offer.

Bathing was, of course, one of the main activities to

take place at Southsea. However, a sense of decorum was a major concern for those who remained firmly attached to Victorian principles. It was not until 1910 that Portsmouth City Council allowed mixed bathing to take place on the beaches. This eventually paved the way for a gradual relaxation of the moral codes defining 'decency' and Southsea can now boast of having a designated area for nude sunbathing.

I remember my brother going in the water. He had a pair of shorts on, but, it wasn't allowed in those days. He had to take them off because the beach inspector came round... [he] could not go in at all, not unless he had a proper bathing costume to cover everything up... the beach

hours out there. (*Jack Price, 1930s*)

We used to swim near enough all year round in the 'bunny' at Sally Port 'cos it was hot... it was only the kids from Portsea who had the balls to do it! We used to get down there and show off and swim in the 'bunny' 'cos the hot water from the power station would come out through there... You'd sort of kid the visitors that you could swim in any weird water! (*Michael Hancock, 1950s*)

In 1976, it was the hottest summer ever and me and my friend skived off school for about three weeks and spent all of our time at the beach. The stones were so hot that they were difficult to walk on with bare feet. We had these fantastic suntans but, of course, when we finally went back to school we were in serious trouble because it was fairly apparent that we had not been away from school because we were ill! It was a glorious time, though, and it was worth all those detentions! (*Eva Balogh, 1970s*)

Although there was no 'Jaws' roaming Southsea waters, there were other potential dangers lurking!

We used to go to Eastney beach, mostly at weekends. All the family used to meet, my aunts and uncles and cousins. We used to have the tents up and we would go out into the sea... have your meals and be there all day. On one occasion we were all sitting all around the tents, and

Swimmers at the landing place near the Sally Port, 1955. (By courtesy of *The News*)

inspector was very fussy in those days. (*Vera Roberts, 1920s*)

I wore a one-piece swimsuit... when they got wet, they drooped!... I had a black top with green trousers. It was like a bodysock... You put it on and pulled the trousers up over the

top, like shorts. (*Ellen Louise (Joe) Hickey, 1930s*)

I used to go out to the beach and swim. In those days there was a diving board they used to winch up and down with the tide – a diving board on wheels. And, there was a raft. I spent many

Beach tents and deckchairs hired from the council at Eastney, 1955. (By courtesy of *The News*)

two liners went by at speed and we all got washed out! It was a wonder no one was drowned. From then on the liners were not allowed to go over a certain speed. It was quite sudden... everybody was afloat! (*Anon, 1930s*)

There were numerous other forms of pleasure to be gained from Southsea seafront besides swimming.

One night a week there was a firework display off the pier [South Parade] and a dance on the pier which you had to pay to go in, but I and a few friends used to climb along the under-works of the pier till we reached the front. When we reached the steps we could climb up on the pier. Then we wriggled between people's feet until we were in the front row for the firework display. One day my friend got caught, he was the last one to climb on and the policeman took him home and told his mother; and his mother told my mother and that stopped that little escapade for a long while! (*Jack Price, teenager in the 1930s*)

We used to build things, model boats and what-have-you, out of old scraps of wood and go and take them down to Canoe Lake and float them down there. (*David Reeves, 1950s*)

We were out one balmy night along Southsea Front and we went to Clarence Pier. It must have been about April-May because the weather was rather nice... and we met these two young men walking on Clarence Pier... these men kept following us and in the end we landed up with them and we went to the top of the Esplanade for a gin and lime... that was my first gin and lime I had, price ninepence.

It nearly broke him! (*Pat Lake, on meeting her husband shortly before World War Two*)

But not everyone could see the seafront's appeal!

My parents used to take me to the seafront.It wasn't a particularly delightful experience but, it was somewhere to go. You used to sit on the seafront and get sand in your sandwiches... The seaside did not appear to be very organised at Portsmouth but a lot of people used to go... sit down there and watch the boats go in and out... the whole thing was entirely bizarre. I found it a little bit of a frightening place, to be honest with you. The horses on the carousels were always garish. I didn't like the funfair at all. (*Terry Chase, 1950s–'60s*)

Equally, for many, Southsea's resort role meant being able earn a living. Hotels, cafeterias, the funfair, the piers and the ice-cream stalls were just some of the places that provided employment.

I used to be outside selling the postcards.... saucy postcards and ordinary ones... and ice-creams then, singing *Tiptoe Through the Tulips* – that had just come out and it was lovely. And the Schneider Cup Trophy [international air races] was on when we were there, which was quite exciting. It brought crowds and crowds – the common was full of people... I used to work from nine until about eight in the evening. (*Vera Roberts worked at the Lifeboat Teahouse, on*

Clarence Esplanade, in 1929, earning 10s (50p) a week).

'Save the last dance for me'

Of all the leisure pursuits that Portsmouth has offered, dancing most surely be one of the most dominant and influential. Whether they provided a waltz or a jitterbug, a pogo or a disco, Portsmouth's dance venues have always been able to oblige. Although purpose-built dance halls, such as the Empress Ballroom or the Savoy, were hugely-popular places to meet, smaller venues, particularly the Southsea bandstand, the local church hall, social and youth clubs and, of course, the 'works dance' were equally important. In addition, and perhaps most significantly, dances were often the place to meet a partner.

That was another 'wicked' thing I used to do, dance every night if I could! I met my husband at the Empress Ballroom dance hall... I could see him coming up the stairs, and I looked at him, and he looked at me, and he asked me to dance. (*Betty Sayers, 1930s*)

A friend of mine said "let's go to St Joseph's Church Hall because they have dances there on a Sunday night" and that was where I first met Ann (my wife)... These two girls came in and my friend and I said "there's two girls on their own" and we went and asked them for a dance... That was a really good social event... We used to go every other Sunday. (*David Hayward, 1950s–'60s*)

I was always out dancing at the pier and at the Savoy, and many other ballrooms. And, of course, my sister was the same. She used to like to go dancing but then, you only paid about threepence to dance round the bandstand or

The bandstand on Southsea Common, where Jack and Dorothy Price met.

the Castle Tea House... We had the Rumba, the Foxtrot, the Slow Foxtrot, the Quickstep, the Tango... We danced at the pier to Wally Fry and his dance band... Dances finished from about ten to half-past ten and the last dance they always played was *Who's Taking You Home Tonight?*... Extremely wonderful dancers were navy dancers... There was nothing like dancing with a sailor! (*Pat Lake, 1940s*)

In the first half of the century a sense of decorum and moral conduct was very much observed, particularly at the local church hall.

You were never allowed to get very close to your partner. If they thought you'd got too close, they'd shout at you from the stage!... You were not allowed alcohol, we had cola, coffee, lemonade or squash. (*David Hayward, 1950s–'60s*)

The other thing, was Saturday afternoons at Kimbells, tea dancing... My mother and father would never go, but one of my friend's parents used to go and sit at the table. There were about five of us about my age, 16-17, and, we used to sit there and have tea and, yes, these young men would come up and ask us to dance. That was our great excitement! And, at six 'o'clock, it was all over and we were taken home! But, just once or twice, when they [the parents] weren't looking, we used to dance a little, outside, and have just the most silly innocuous kiss. (*Sheila Duce, 1940s*)

Sheila Duce, 1943.

Dancing, as with all aspects of the leisure industry, also provided a huge pool of employment opportunities. Dances had to be organised, a band had to be hired and steps had to be learnt.

I became secretary to the social section, and I was obliged to run so many dances a year. We hired the Oddfellows Hall in Fratton Road as the venue and a three-piece orchestra, which I seem to remember was a fiddle, a saxophone and a piano, used to come and play. And, we had tea and buns or sandwiches halfway through... They would start about seven and end about nine... with a break mid-way through to have the refreshments. A very simple affair. (*Jack Price, social secretary of 'The Telegraph Boys', 1930s*)

I did go dancing as an amateur and I took my bronze, silver and gold amateur dancing medals... I went to Southsea for a course of lessons and I took my Associateship – teacher's, that is... and with my amateur dancing partner, Frank Isherwood, we decided to try and start a school of dancing... It went off like a bomb! We had loads of people coming for lessons... there were loads of dances everywhere and, we put people through for their medals; we trained them for competitions and we adjudicated and judged. (*Ivy Tibbles, founder of The Ivy Hadley School of Dancing, 1940s–'50s*)

During the last 50 years, dancing has experienced a radical transformation. The popularity of the traditional formal dance, such as the waltz, was successfully challenged by rock 'n' roll and the 'birth' of the teenager during the 1950s. From this period, the record industry advanced at a phenomenal rate and eventually, with the creation of the disc jockey, the live band was no longer the necessary accompaniment to dancing. 'Clubbing' was born and has remained as popular as the traditional dance halls.

We usually went to Nero's. It was a very strange place really. It had an elevated dance floor that had lights flashing on it and statues of... well, I suppose they were of Nero. There were always a few girls who were 'showy-off'

Ivy Hadley presenting a dancing trophy, about 1950.

dancers but me and my friends weren't really interested in that sort of dancing. We just loved Disco! Lots of soul and, of course, the women's anthem, *I Will Survive* by Gloria Gaynor. During the '80s, we tended to go to a small club in North End, called Gatsby's and Martine's, that used to be the old Palace Cinema. We would go dancing two or three times a week and get up for work the next day! (*Eva Balogh, 1970s–'80s*)

If you didn't manage to get in the nightclub, there was always the local youth club.

Girls would turn up at the youth clubs, so you met them there, jiving round to the records... You got quite a few girls jived together, handbags down on the floor and dancing around it! Actually the fellas didn't jive at first, they probably thought it was a bit sissy but eventually most of the guys ended up jiving! (*David Gamblen, 1950s*)

The youth club was the place to go, every Friday. The one I went to was Trinity Methodist at the end of Francis Avenue. It was the most popular, because you didn't have to go to church, whereas St Jude's, you had to go to church

at least three times a month otherwise you were kicked out of the youth club!... they used to put on functions, like discos... it was a place where the music was played quite loud and, there was a little bar. You only had soft drinks or crisps, but it was somewhere we could go and be ourselves. (*Jackie Bryden, 1970s*)

Dancing still remains a popular leisure activity and the abundance of nightclubs in Portsmouth testifies to this. Clubbing is a part of many people's lives and nightclubs still retain some of the traditional aspects of the

A 'Dancing to Health' demonstration in the Guildhall during the 1930s.

past dance halls. That is, people dance, have fun and meet partners.

I now go to Decadence on a Saturday night, which is in the Pyramids at Southsea. We go there because they play really good music – Hard House, Trance – and they have four different rooms in there that play different sorts of music. We sometimes go in to Buddy's which is a 'retro' room. They play '60s/'70s/'80s music. It is expensive to get in and expensive to drink in there, so we usually get drunk before

we go so we don't have to buy any drinks there. It is £7.00 to get in or £8.00 if they have a well-known DJ, and they charge £3.40 for a bottle of Smirnoff Ice! But it is a good place to meet men... I met my boyfriend there. (*Layla Garner, 1990s–2000*)

Gunwharf Quays has a nice night-club, Tiger, Tiger. They have different rooms for different tastes. You can dance, chill, eat, or just listen to the music. It seems to attract older people, which is good because many of the other clubs in Portsmouth are

full of under-21s... And although I like to dance, always have done, I find it difficult to dance to some of the music that they play... And, I have met a couple of nice men there! (*Jackie Bryden, 1990s–2000*)

'Fancy a night in?'

Leisure activities have not always been pursued outside of the home environment. Card games, board games, and toys have always featured heavily in children's lives. Equally, reading, gardening or DIY have found their way in to the long list of home-based activities. However, of all the 'at home' leisure pursuits, radio and television were, undoubtedly, the two most significant and influential forms of home entertainment to emerge during the last century. Acting as both communicator and entertainer, these two forms of media have developed into powerful institutions. Furthermore, advances in technology have created a home-based computer leisure industry that is growing at an incredible rate.

They [the BBC] transmitted songs, music... father would be sitting in the front room playing with his crystal set with this headphones on and, somebody would come dashing in and shut the door and, he's lost his programme because the 'cat whisker' had

jumped off the crystal and he'd swear at his youngsters! So, he took his crystal set up to the bedroom to get away from the family! (*Laurie Upton, 1920s*)

We spent a lot of time listening to plays on the radio... Sunday lunch-time was a ritual... We always got home for Cliff Michelmore's *Family Favourites*. And then, at one o'clock was Billy Cotton... after that came *Educating Archie* and, after that, was *Down Your Way*... Saturday was Tommy Handley... and sausages! We always had sausages on Saturday and we had to have them at the time Tommy Handley was on the radio! (*Ann Hayward, 1940s–'50s*)

One Christmas, I got given a small radio which had an earpiece attachment. How fantastic! That meant I could listen to the radio in bed without anyone else hearing it! Always listened to Radio Luxembourg

because they played all the pop songs at the time and, of course, it seemed a bit rebellious listening to a commercial station rather than Radio One. I've got a feeling they even played Donna Summer's *Love to Love You Baby* after the BBC banned it from Radio One. I often woke up in the morning with the ear-piece in my ear! (*Eva Balogh, 1970s*)

The radio used to be on all the time, through most of the day. I remember on Sunday evenings, doing my homework in the kitchen and listening to 'The Chart'. It used to on Radio One... if we started singing along to it, we got told off because obviously we weren't concentrating on our homework enough and, it would get turned off! So, you had to listen and not sing! (*Gina Garner, 1970s*)

The radio then, has been an important entertainer since its birth, and still continues to provide pleasure for many people. Perhaps one of its big advantages is its portability unlike its great rival, the television set, at first a luxury item.

I remember we were quite late in having a TV set... about 1957... we watched *Cheyenne*, which was the first thing I ever saw, which was a cowboy. And, I can see us all now, clustered round this Ultra set and, it transformed your life! Especially when you were a child... and, no doubt all our neighbour's lives because some nights you wouldn't see any children in the street! (*Ernest Aspey, 1950s*)

Pete Young's Radio One show broadcast live from the Odeon Cinema, about 1968.

The Waverley Hockey club, Southsea, photographed in 1918. The men are soldiers wearing hospital uniform.

There was one family down the street that had a television set and this television set was fitted with an ear-phone so that granny could hear what was going on. I have this vivid memory of going into this house on a Saturday morning, which was the only time when all the other kids were allowed in, and there would be about 20 or 30 children in this house and we would all be sitting round this television set watching a programme. And, granny would be stuck up in the corner with her hearing aid plugged into it. It was almost like going to the pictures because in the middle of the morning this guy's mum used to come round with biscuits and lemonade. It was great fun! (*David Reeves, 1950s*)

I remember the first time we got a colour TV. It was put in the front room, not the living room, which still had the black and white set. We were all allowed in the front room to have a look at this colour set! It must have been a Saturday because the programme showing was *Stingray* and I remember seeing Marina, the mermaid, in glorious colour! (*Eva Balogh, young in the 1960s–'70s*)

But, television viewing has changed dramatically during the last 20 years. It is now available 24 hours a day, seven days a week. Cable and satellite systems have brought with them a further influx of American programmes that have become hugely popular, particularly with teenagers.

I watch a lot of telly, a lot...

Nickelodeon, [which shows] *Sister, Sister*... Trouble, which has got *USA High*, *California Dreams* and others like that... *Jerry Springer*, I like that because its got loads of swearing and violence in it, it's just funny... It's a chat show which has all different things on it and people fight, but they 'bleep' the swearing out... When it's on late at night I think they should leave it in! (*Layla Garner, teenager, 1990s*)

Advances in technology have created an explosion in home-based leisure activities. The designated games computer is now a common 'toy' for many children (and adults). Equally, the personal computer is fast becoming not only a tool for work, but the system through which an

The dancefloor around the Southsea Common bandstand was turned first into a roller-skating rink and then in the 1980s into a skate park.

international leisure activity can take place.

I built my own personal computer and use it for lots of things. I play games on it and use the internet a lot to find out lots of information. I can download music from web sites, see what is on at the cinema, and generally find out anything I want to know the answer to. The latest game I bought is called *Black and White*. Basically, you are God and you make decisions about what to do with 'your people'. You can decide to blow them all up or create a tidal wave and destroy them. At the end, depending on what you have done, you will be judged as good or evil [black side or white side]. It's a good game. (*William Harvey, teenager, 1990s*)

I do like going on the internet, that's my latest thing, that's good

fun... Last week I was on the internet every day, but usually it's at least once a week to chat in chat rooms and to speak to my friends if they happen to be 'on-line'... lots of Americans generally... You can quite easily spend two hours chatting on the Net... At the weekends, a two-hour call is only going to cost £1.00... it's certainly cheaper that going to night-clubs or pubs, though I suppose you could argue that it can be quite isolating but, you get to chat to lots of different people all over the world... and... you can be anyone you want to be on the internet! (*Gina Garner, 1990s*)

'Fancy a drink?'

Socialising over glass of wine, a pint of beer or a cup of tea or coffee is a long-standing tradition. Public

houses have long been the venue to partake of alcohol and often, a bite to eat. Portsmouth has, for centuries, been able to offer an enormous selection of pubs and, in recent years, wine bars have become extremely popular. As with pubs, Portsmouth has had a number of coffee bars that thrived as venues for both young and old. The influence of America in the 1950s helped the rise in coffee bar culture because so many installed the latest jukebox. Thus coffee bars, and in particular cafés, became synonymous with youth or teenager culture, providing an adult environment without the 'over 18' restriction.

Coffee bars? They were great! They had these enormous espresso coffee machines on the counter that made a hell of a racket! There seemed to be all sorts of levers to pull behind them. Lots of gushing and sort of whirling sounds and water having to be topped up here and steam let off there and it almost felt as if you needed to be a train driver to operate one of those coffee machines!... In fact, I hated espresso coffee! I found that after two cups I felt decidedly ill but, of course, if you wanted to stay in the coffee bar all evening there was only a certain amount of time you could get away with having only just one cup of coffee. (*David Reeves, young in the 1950s–'60s*)

LEISURE, PLEASURE AND ENTERTAINMENT

You used to go to the coffee bars not as a means to an end but as an end to the evening... We used to go to the pubs in Southsea, then when they used to close at 11 o'clock, we would go to the coffee bars. There were two in Osborne Road that we used to go to. One was called the Bistro, which tended to be more packed and lively and, they had a juke box in there. And, the other one was Del Monaco's... sometimes we used to go in to them, especially the Bistro, and never buy anything... but we never used to get thrown out because it was so packed! (*Terry Chase, young in the 1960s*)

Of all the coffee bars in Portsmouth, one of the most well known and, perhaps the most popular, was Verrecchia's. Opening in 1933, with its distinctive seating booths, delicious coffee and, of course, its famous knickerbocker glories, Verrecchia's remains a landmark in the history of Portsmouth's coffee bars. It finally closed in 1970 when Guildhall Square was redeveloped.

Their ice-creams – you could have raspberry sauce on it – I don't know how they did it but their ice-cream always tasted different to anybody else's... You could get these big knickerbocker glories, right down to the bottom of the glass, all this lovely fruit... and there was always a cherry on the top. He [her husband] never used to get his because I liked the cherries and he didn't! (*Evelyn*

The compere and contestants of a beauty contest organised by *The Sunday Pictorial*, 1958.

Ruth Tickner, customer in the 1940s)

Verrecchia's wasn't a café, it was more of a coffee house... a meeting point prior to going to the Guildhall for a concert or going down to the Savoy... You could sit in the alcoves there and watch the people go by... it was the hub of Portsmouth. (*Dave Gamblen, customer, 1950s & '60s*)

So, what was the secret of their success?

That was my grandfather's job, to make the mixed fruit, and we used to make it in this great big stainless steel bowl. Dad would never buy anything that was already done. He said it was never quite the same as if you had done it fresh... [To make a knickerbocker glory] You put some jelly in the bottom, a bit of

The Sussex Hotel, Guildhall Square, in 1953.

ice-cream on top, then some fruit, some more ice-cream, then some more fruit... it was always done with vanilla ice-cream... and then put a cherry on the top and then, put this gorgeous raspberry syrup over it. (*Lidia Briano, proprietor's daughter, Verrecchia's*)

An alternative to the coffee bar would be the café. Often with a juke box, cafés established themselves as a popular (and cheap) meeting place for young people.

If we came in to town [Portsmouth] a very popular place was the Hot-Dog in Kingston Crescent. That was unique because it was a very narrow frontage that went back a long way, like a corridor, with seats and booths and a long bar... You'd go in there, order your cup of tea and a roll... at the very end was a jukebox with a very small floor where you could actually dance... so, you could play rock 'n' roll music and jive. (*Dave Gamblen, café customer, 1950s–'60s*)

American-style 'fast food' has become dominant since the 1970s. Burgers and fries, shakes and cola have become the popular alternative to coffee and ice-cream. Although there are still many cafes remaining in Portsmouth, it is more likely that the young will now eat, drink and socialise in a 'Mac-donald's' or a 'Burger King'.

The Duke of Cornwall, 1946, one of Portsmouth's many backstreet 'locals'.

Instead of walking along the sea-front or hanging around in the parks, we moved off to 'the Wimpy' where we used to have things like knickerbocker glories and burgers because they [burger bars] had just started opening then... it was new thing in town... it was in Palmerston Road in Southsea. (*Jackie Bryden, teenager, 1970s*)

If I go in to Portsmouth, I go in to Macdonald's. It's not expensive because you can get a 'two-pounder', which is two burgers and two fries for £2.00... then you can share it with your friends. (*Layla Garner, 1990s*)

Of course, coffee or cola is no substitute for a beer or a glass of wine!

The local pub was the Avenue Hotel... which had a children's room... my parents did take us up there on occasion... if we had been out – perhaps to the park... my dad would get a pint of beer and my mother would have a half of shandy, we had lemonade and would sit in the children's room. (*Ernest Aspey, young in the 1950s*)

We used to go out sometimes on a Sunday, we used to go for a long walk and then we used to go in a pub for a drink. (*Margaret Herridge, young in the 1940s–'50s*)

If they [the parents] went to the pub, if there wasn't a family room then I'd sort of have to stay outside, but that didn't happen

very often. The Mermaid down the bottom of the road had a family room, so I could go in there. Although they would generally 'abandon' me in there with the snooker table or whatever was in there and they would go in to the main bar... I could always see them through the hatch, so it wasn't a problem. (*Terry Chase, young in the 1950s*)

I'm a regular at Rosie's [wine bar] in Elm Grove. I've been going there for about 20 years now, so I'm a bit of a regular! They often have jazz bands playing and you can get a decent bottle of wine in there. It's a very sociable place. (*Jackie Bryden, 1990s*)

We tend to go to Wetherspoon's at Cosham or Havant, primarily

Inside the Keppel's Head in 1952, a hotel on the Hard popular with naval officers.

and the workplace, football is probably the most evident and perhaps the most popular. And, for many "Play up Pompey" is the only chant to sing on a Saturday afternoon!

Anyone who prides themselves on being a 'Portsmouthian' supports Pompey football club! I used to go there and my grandfather used to take me from about the age of seven... The atmosphere was really good even when they went down in to the Third Division. (*Terry Chase, Pompey supporter, 1950s–'70s*)

First time I watched them play was, I think, 1929, when I was eight years old... on big matches there would be 20,000. It was a regular gate in those days... Most of the support came from locals... In those days everybody had their special spot, so at 12 o'clock the gates used to open and in they used to rush to grab their

because they are cheap! We also go to Guildhall Square where there are now lots of pubs and bars. We go to Bar Me, Yates' and The Mucky Duck [The White Swan]. I usually drink 'Stella' [strong lager] but my friend tends to drink 'alcopops'. (*Layla Garner, 1990s*)

I have a group of girlfriends that I have known for around 20 years. We always see each other on a Friday night and usually drink rather a lot of wine! We like to try out a variety of places. We often do an 'Eastney run' which means starting at the Alma Arms and finishing somewhere in Albert Road! We also go to the pubs at North End, Havant and Stamshaw. As long as they are friendly and sell decent wine, we don't really mind what they are like! (*Anonymous, 1980s–'90s*)

'It's not the winning, it's the taking part...'

Whether partaking or viewing, sport is, for many,

an essential part of leisure time. There is a plethora of sporting activities available in Portsmouth, which include cricket, squash, badminton, tennis, working out at the gym, running and athletics. However, with a well-known professional football team and an abundance of amateur football leagues made up of teams from schools, pubs

Celebrating Pompey's return to Division One, 1987. (By courtesy of *The News*)

spots! (*Ken Bell, supporter and turnstile-man, 1929–'98*)

I used to go to Fratton park, a shilling a time. Quite often I went with my friends. Portsmouth, at that time, were in the First Division [then the top-flight]... We used to go quite early, they'd open the gates at one o'clock and you could go right down to the front on the terraces... take a pile of comics with you and read them and stand on them, if you had to, to see over the wall!... It wasn't unusual for a youngster to be passed down through the crowd to somewhere down the front! (*Terry Butler, young Pompey supporter, 1950s–'60s*)

Tickets for two of Portsmouth Football Club's FA Cup Finals at Wembley between the wars.

Aside from winning the Football League Championship in 1948-9 and 1940-50, probably Portsmouth's most famous moment was when they won the FA Cup Final in 1939, with a score of 4-1 against Wolverhampton Wanderers. And, as a result of World War Two they retained the cup for seven years!

You walk out of that tunnel on to the ground and, there is 100,000 screaming! You are just in another world really. You just can't explain it... the happiest memory was when I kicked the first goal in... and then it was even better when Jock Anderson poured one in, right into the top corner and made it two-nil! And we came out second-half and we were another in front after a few seconds, three-none up! Wembley was unbelievable! Then we gave an exhibition really because Wolves were finished. They pulled one back but we slotted another in and that made it four and nobody would have believed it that we could play as well as that! (*Bert Barlow, Pompey player in the FA Cup Final, 1939*)

For others, the FA Cup Final is remembered for entirely different reasons.

We had arranged our marriage for the day of the Cup Final, although we didn't know that Portsmouth would be in it at the time. So, when Portsmouth got through to the Final we had to postpone the wedding until the following day because Norman [her husband] had tickets for the

match! The only reason I minded a bit was because on the day of the match it was really nice weather but the next day, for our wedding, it was raining and really miserable! (*Ellen Louise (Joe) Hickey, Pompey supporter*)

However, there is life beyond football!

I adored playing cricket and I played cricket for a long time but, again, I wasn't very good at it! But it's the sort of thing that a lot of enthusiasm can get you a lot further, because chasing a ball over a park and throwing the ball in was a decent contribution to the game! Cricket was the main thing I used to play. (*Terry Chase, cricket player, 1960s–'70s*)

And the growth of the 'leisure centre' in recent years has provided a variety of sporting recreation.

I play badminton once a week with a group of friends. I like to think it makes me fitter but... well, it's a good way of seeing friends as well. It's also quite cheap. (*Jackie Bryden, 1990s*)

I used to play squash and badminton a regular basis, two or three times a week when I was younger. I also used to go to the gym, but sport is not so appealing nowadays! Perhaps I just don't have the time! I do walk a lot though, so, that's my exercise! (*Anonymous, 1980s*)

I go to the gym two or three times a week. I find it really exhilarating! My sons also go to

Airspeed's cricket team, probably in the 1950s.

the gym. In fact, it was them that got me started! It's a great stress reliever! (*Anonymous, 1990s*)

We go to the Pyramids. It's a swimming centre, well, you can do a bit of swimming but it's really a fun pool. They've got waves every 15 minutes and pipes that you can go down... I also go to Victoria Swimming Baths where you can really swim properly. I sometimes go to the beach to swim when the weather is okay. (*Miles Balogh, teenager, 1990s*)

We liked the country... Bikes of course... I think that's what kept us fit, cycling... We would cycle to Rowlands Castle, Fort Widley... over the hill. (*George and Evelyn Tickner, cyclists 1930s–'50s*)

For some, cycling became both a recreation and a serious sport.

I joined the Cyclists Touring Club

in 1934... we would cycle for 12 hours, sometimes, and cover about 65 miles... it was nothing for us to ride from Cosham, starting at nine o'clock and we would ride to Lyndhurst in the New Forest... We used to go to a

place called the Swan Inn at Emery Down... we would have lunch there and then, during the afternoon, we would cycle through the New Forest and... probably come back to Petersfield for tea and then home... it would just make a very nice day out! (*Bill Harmsworth, cyclist, 1930s–'90s*)

And, cycling is still seen as a very good way to get round the New Forest!

The other week we got the train to Brockenhurst because we wanted to go to the New Forest. The only way to get round it properly was to walk or ride a bike. We hired bikes and cycled for about 15 miles! Cycling is great but as we hadn't done it for a while we had some aches and pains for a few days! (*William Harvey, teenager, 1990s*)

Portsmouth North End Cycling Club on an outing, 1907.

THE FACE OF PORTSMOUTH

John Stedman

NOT only has the way the people of Portsmouth live their lives changed radically during the 20th century, but the physical character of the city, its streets and buildings, has changed dramatically, too. There are three interlinked themes.

Everybody has been touched by improvements in housing conditions. In 1900 there were many homes without even a cold water tap. Most houses were heated by open coal fires. Electric lighting was still rare, gas lights were usual, but sometimes were provided only downstairs. As late as 1970, 12.1 per cent of homes in Portsmouth had only an outside toilet and more than 6 per cent lacked a bath. In 2002 it is unusual for new houses to be built without central heating or double-glazing. As people have grown more prosperous, they have been able to demand higher standards or buy their own homes, while the council undertook a long campaign of demolishing and redeveloping slum houses, constructing well-built houses for rent.

Second, the town of Portsmouth has grown in area. In 1900 the built-up area covered only the western side of Portsea Island, including Fratton, North

A flood in Broad Street, Point, in 1910.

End and parts of Stamshaw and Eastney. By 1920 it embraced most of the south and east of Portsea Island also and, in the following two decades, Portsmouth expanded across Hilsea, Wymering, Cosham and Drayton, absorbing the existing villages. After the war came new housing estates at Paulsgrove, and then the council built beyond the city boundaries at Leigh Park, Crookhorn and Wecock Farm.

Third, there has been major reshaping of the older areas of Portsmouth. Wartime German bombing, which destroyed or badly damaged a fifth of the city's buildings and devastated three of its main shopping areas, was the most obvious cause. But there were other factors. One was the council's policy of replacing older, sub-standard housing with better, less-crowded homes, which began in 1911 with the creation of Curzon Howe Road and Portsmouth's first council houses. Another was the spread of the car, demanding improved roads. A third was the run-down of Portsmouth as a garrison town. The redundant barracks and fortifications have been sold for housing and leisure facilities.

Before World War Two

Much of Portsmouth's housing in the first half of the century was small and often overcrowded.

The rent was 9s 6d [48p] a week, which was a lot of money.... the toilet was right down the back of the garden. We had a scullery

Early 19th-century houses in Ridge Street, Landport, in 1962, typical of Portsmouth's older housing, mostly now demolished.

with an old gas stove and a copper, which you had to light the fire under the bottom of... a very long passage. There was gas downstairs, but only candles upstairs. There was no electricity or nothing like that. And the running water, that was a tap out in the scullery, which was some way away. We had a front room, a back room, with stairs in between. You had stairs going down into a great big cellar... that's where the coal was kept, down there. And then upstairs you had a front room and a back room, and then another set of stairs going up and you had two attics, one on each side. And my mother used to let the attics for about 3 bob [15p] a week to lodgers and that helped pay the rent. (*John Slade who, during the 1920s and '30s was brought up in a house in Orange Street, Portsea, next to a slaughterhouse. In 1935 it was pulled down to make way for flats*)

In the oldest parts of the town, Old Portsmouth and

Portsea, where there were small houses in narrow courtyards behind the street frontages, conditions were the worst in Portsmouth.

We used to live up an alleyway and then, I suppose, it was a big

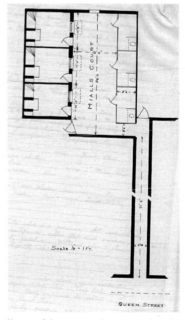
Houses of three storeys, but rooms only 10ft by 9ft 9 in (3.7m by 3 m), in Mialls Court, off Queen Street. They were demolished in 1929 as unfit for habitation.

yard, and then there was the six houses along. It was just one bedroom, up and down, and the tap was in the middle of this place, and then I remember we had a... 'wash-house' they used to call it then, with a copper and all that, and you used to hang your washing up in there, and they had six toilets along the back... We each [family] had our own one. The seats was, you know, all scrubbed – all wooden seats... They weren't very big, there was one big bed and another bed... we all slept in the same room. (*Resident of Pills Place, off Havant Street, in the 1920s*)

Many a family found itself in straightened circumstances in the late 1920s.

I think we had two rooms and the use of the kitchen... My mother lost quite a few children before I was born. There was my brother Charlie, there was myself came next, my sister Ivy, my brother Alf and my brother Ron. And in the bedroom there was a double bed and a single bed. Now, we all slept in there. I mean, I was very young but I knew all about a boy's body when I was very young, because there was no privacy. Mother and father slept in the bed with a couple of kids with them and one down the end, and then we slept top to tail... And, of course, the jerry pot was in there as well. I mean you all used it because the toilet was outside in... it wasn't a garden, it was a yard... you didn't dream of going down in the night. We used the jerry. All of

us! Thinking about it now, it must have been dreadful. (*Gladys Fisher remembering family life after her father lost his job.*)

Housing and businesses were intermingled. Circus animals were stabled in the yard under Gladys Fisher's flat in Landport, for example, while next door was a greengrocer, with his horse and cart:

... and there was Cuthbert's, the milkman, with his horse and trap, and his milk trap, and there was Mr Glew with his blacksmith's, and there was George Cooper [a butcher] with his store with the live animals, and his slaughterhouse at the end, all in this community. It was like living in the middle of the country. (*Gladys Fisher*)

Many houses suffered from damp and infestation.

But of course in those houses... we weren't the only living creatures that lived there... These places were alive, alive with bugs. And my Mum, every Friday, would do that house from top to bottom... And my dear old mum used to go round to a chemist in Lake Road, name of Fox, and used to buy two twopenny tubs of bug... Keatings bug powder. Plus the fact we used to boil the water up then take it upstairs, and she would pour the boiling water all over the ends of the beds and bed frames and spray the powder on the walls. My dad, he wouldn't have any wallpaper, he pasted the walls with lead paint, to restrict

the bugs. (*Frank Deacon, brought up in Landport in the 1920s*)

Even before World War Two growing motor traffic was causing problems. Fratton Road was widened in 1929, causing at least temporary difficulties for local tradesmen.

... it ruined everybody's business in Fratton Road. They couldn't do any trade, you see. The road was messed up. The people couldn't come in there to do their shopping, so it ruined their damned business. I remember I used to serve the printers called Lloyds down Fratton Road, served them for years, you know. Of course, we lost them, couldn't get there to serve them, you see. (*Robert Benham, dairyman 1919–55*)

There were unusual and unexpected features of the townscape everywhere, such as on Broad Street:

Mr Wyllie [W.L. Wyllie, the marine artist, who lived in Tower House on Point]... he was a firm friend. He'd touch us on the head as he went past us, sort of "I've noticed you". And then the old tram stables was at the bottom of the lane that led up to Tower House. It wasn't used, not in my lifetime, as a tram stables, but [you could tell] it was because the original tramlines were still there. He took that and he made it into a magnificent museum for his paintings. I went in there on one of my trips down... and it was beautiful... he had them all

The first aircraft to land at Portsmouth airfield, before the site was fully cleared, 15 December 1930. Hilsea gasworks is in the background. (By courtesy of *The News*)

on easels there. (*Eileen Rayner, resident of Point*)

Suburban development, turning fields into rows of houses, had long been under way by 1914, and it continued after World War One. The Highbury estate was the largest of the new estates and was advertised heavily throughout the 1930s. A generously-proportioned terraced house there cost £595.

I came in in the March, and he [her elder son] was born in the May... they were marvellous houses. I was over the moon, I thought it was marvellous, the round corners, you know, the fireplaces... you could have a hot water system or you could have a shed... I wanted the bathroom tiled halfway up... In the kitchen you had a gas boiler, you had a cupboard with an ironing board, you had a big – wash-up with a butler sink and a door to shut everything off from the kitchen.

Then you had a dresser... they had tea and all in porcelain [storage containers] and they had "Highbury Houses" on... the door to the larder, that had a cupboard on to keep your brushes and all that in... There's this [living] room, dining room, kitchen, bathroom, three bedrooms, big bedroom. Even the small bedroom – my son's got a house at Crawley and his biggest bedroom is not much bigger than my little bedroom. (*Mrs Eileen Booker who bought one of the Highbury estate houses with her husband, a petty officer in the navy, in 1936*)

There were also council houses built at Cosham in the 1920s.

Well, that was very nice. When we first went up there, the farmyard was still there at the bottom of Wymering Lane. There was still a farm there, and a duck-pond and all that sort of thing. The house was like a normal house now. It was a three-bedroom council house with a bathroom and all the usual, with a nice bit of garden back and front. That was very nice. (*Anonymous, moved to Cosham in the mid-1920s*)

A variety of housing types sprung up throughout the area and many families were happy to move into better accommodation.

Well, it was totally different. We

Houses at Hawthorn Crescent under construction, about 1936.

Portsmouth's first council houses, Curzon Howe Road, with a bathroom, but an outside toilet, built 1911–13.

had a bath. I know in Bridport Street we had the galvanised tub, which was in front of the two-bar electric fire. I can feel the heat of the fire now from when I was about four or five years old. We had an Ascot water heater, a multi-point, which gave you constant hot water. You had an inside WC, where in Bridport Street it was an outside outhouse. You can imagine the scene in winter, it was frozen and pretty grim, especially when you were about 4 years old – in the middle of the night being taken down there. I had my own bedroom – you know we all had to sleep in a multi – in a bedsitter... It was a great thing. We had two bedrooms, a living room, kitchen, a larder and a proper bathroom and toilet, so it was a great improvement. I mean, bear in mind that these houses were built in the 1920s so they were already 30 years old, but compared with Bridport Street they were a fantastic improvement... we had gardens at Bridport Street but they were never our own, they

were shared... we had our own garden at the rear. Back in the '50s my father kept chickens, he decided that he wanted to keep chickens... but this was not particularly unusual in the 50s. (*Ernest Aspey and his family moved from a two-room flat in a converted Victorian house to a 1920s, purpose-built, two-bedroom flat in Childe Square, Stamshaw in 1951*)

Reconstruction

The war transformed Portsmouth's townscape. Shortages of materials, skilled manpower and national economic difficulties conspired to make the reconstruction slow, while the council decided to concentrate on providing homes rather than rebuilding the blitzed city centre. The first houses were built in 1946 and the first shop in Commercial Road – C & A – reopened in 1952.

At that time [1946] the ration of timber for any one job was £1... you didn't get much timber for £1, so if you were out jobbing, you might say – one instance was in Winter Road, a house in Winter Road – repair the floor. You were expected to cut little bits out between the joists... patch up the floor with bits of board, which never made a job, never a satisfactory job... and it was quite time-consuming. (*Ken Freemantle, carpenter 1939–89*)

We moved into that place and we were one of the earlier houses to be built down there [Old Portsmouth, the only part of the city to be zoned for private housing in the reconstruction plan], and we moved in in 1953. The war'd been won in 1945, so that was longer, far longer, half as long again as the war itself! (*Pat Haskell, purchaser of a newly built house, 1953*)

There was a great deal of building work to be done after the war.

All the builders, all the builders in Pompey was after us to replace stonework. They were all getting the money through the government, you see... we were everywhere replacing stone... We had as many as 32 masons in our yard working, at the time, just after the war... Oh, but the buildings! Big buildings. We took the Connaught Drill Hall on, jobs like that; I had the Chamber of Commerce, Westminster Bank, and some of the shops in Commercial Road, all going at the same time. (*Len Kidd, who worked for Marchetti Bros, stonemasons, after World War Two*)

The big Co-op house in Fratton Road had been destroyed by fire and we rebuilt that, which was three storeys. We rebuilt it as it was original, with Portland stone on the outside, and we did that in approximately two years, with our own labour force. At the same time we were building the Co-op dairy in Drayton, which is still there today, and the garage and the bakery which was all in Station Road in Drayton. While that was going on, we were building shops, such as [those] in Paulsgrove... So, up to about 18 months, we started building the big Co-op store which is in Allaway Avenue at the present time. There were shops being built in various parts of Portsmouth by the Co-op, and a lot of the old ones was being refurbished and opened up as, in latter years, self-service. And the Co-op was the first self-service shop in the whole of England. Which was opened in Albert Road in Portsmouth. (*Fred Grist, scaffolder for the Co-op, late 1940s & '50s*)

Immediately after the war the council erected over 700 temporary prefabricated bungalows, on bombsites all over the city, and the slopes of Portsdown Hill. People were loath to leave them.

I lived at 2 Courtmount Grove, and I moved over the other side of the road to 25, to save

Prefabs on Portsdown Hill, photographed about 1947.

moving, because I liked it so much up the prefabs. There was only two bedrooms, a kitchen and a living room [plus a bathroom], but it was nice and comfortable... We were as snug as a bug in a rug up there... that fire we had in the living room kept the whole place warm and dry. (*John Dean, resident of prefabs on Portsdown Hill*)

But the beauty of it was we had a fridge, which was an innovation. Believe you me, that was nice! We had a gas fridge, it had a little pilot jet. What our nippers

was doing was just making ice cream all day – with cornflour! We had a lovely little garden round it. We had top prize for 16 years running... they got fed up with me, I'll tell you!... They were lovely little places, they had a ten-year life. And we were in them 16. They were still good. (*Len Kidd, resident of a prefab*)

New estates of permanent houses were built in Paulsgrove and Leigh Park. For speed, many of the houses erected in Paulsgrove were built using non-traditional methods.

Once you had done one it was all repetition. You put the steel frame up and the chimney, which was steel, and the staircase, which was steel, and then the carpenters would come along and finish the construction and people would put the asbestos roofs and cladding on the sides

New houses in Paulsgrove of both conventional and steel-frame construction, about 1950.

The first shops in Paulsgrove – converted from Nissen huts. (By courtesy of *The News*)

and that. So it was a bit of a really boring job. (*Fred Grist, building worker and resident of Paulsgrove*)

...after I finished on Bailey & Claxons on Canal Walk I went up to Howards at Paulsgrove working on the prefabs... that was the Howard-type prefabs. All sectional floors and precast concrete panels... We would put the floor sections in quite a number, the kitchen units were already prefabricated at Crawley, they were ready built and they were hoisted into place. There would be two kitchens in one unit, which was slung off of the crane, slung in position in the centre of the house and then the steelwork erected around them... We put the floors in and the other gangs would come along and they would put all the cladding on. While they were doing that we would be working on the... barge boards up on the roofs. Simple enough. (*Ken Freemantle, carpenter, 1939–89*)

Most people were delighted with their new council houses, whether in Paulsgrove or Leigh Park, the contrast with their previous living conditions was so great.

Oh, we were over the moon to be able to get a nice house of our own. Start getting a real home together that we had never had before. I mean, I would have been married then about six years and we had never known what it was like to have a place of our own... They were, you know, little palaces, really... (*Fred Grist, resident of Paulsgrove from 1947*)

... my mother, I think, was ecstatic because it was suddenly a home of her own, she'd never had a home of her own, and I think that gave her the freedom to do what she wanted in her home... we moved up there [to Leigh Park] in something like 1954, but it was such a novelty to have our own house and our own garden, and it represented,

like, freedom and colour. I think that's when my childhood took on colour, because it wasn't the drab inner-city feeling, we were suddenly in the country, there were open spaces, there were fields all around us... (*Andrea Burgess, who moved to Leigh Park as a child*)

Facilities were poor at first in both Paulsgrove and Leigh Park.

It was very hard to start with because there were no shops and what used to happen, the Co-op and various people had these mobile shops that would come round your road once or twice a week and he would toot his horn and you went outside to the van and bought what you wanted. Failing that you had to go to Cosham, and there wasn't many big stores in Cosham at that time. There was no public houses here

Mrs Kathleen Newman in Paulsgrove's first fish-and-chip shop, c.1950.

– the nearest public house was the Harbour Lights on Southampton Road... When I moved here there was no schools except for three wooden black huts at the end of Cheltenham Road, Paulsgrove. It was several years that the people living in Paulsgrove – the children – had to go by bus each morning down into Portsmouth to go to school, and eventually they started building the new schools, which was Hillside, Hillview and Castle View, they were the first three permanent schools that was built in Paulsgrove... they got money from the ecclesiastical commissioners and that, and the church was commenced in October 1955. That was when the foundation stone was laid and it was completed in mid-1957. Consecrated in July 1957. The cost of the land and the church and the vicarage was £1,575. (*Fred Grist, building worker and resident of Paulsgrove, recorded in 1994*)

I'm sure everybody was very happy when Leigh Park had its own shopping centre; when there was a Co-op supermarket, and then they built a department store on top of it, and the rest of the shops developed in Park Parade. It didn't satisfy the main shopping requirements if one needed clothing, but basic requirements were provided there. (*Jan Ross, resident of Leigh Park, 1950–74*)

Local building workers had some surprising help.

The roads was constructed,

mostly, by German prisoners-of-war and there used to be a big Polish refugee camp along by Portchester, and these Polish refugees was here, and the German prisoners-of-war were here, for several years doing the roads and the drainage for Paulsgrove. And they were, I think, quite happy to be living and working in Paulsgrove. (*Fred Grist, building worker and resident of Paulsgrove*)

The rebuilding of the commercial areas got under way only slowly.

Yes, Palmerston Road, which was a beautiful shopping centre, was smashed to pieces and we found that they were always deciding on plans and then scrapping it, as opposed to Plymouth... they had a very good building plan for Plymouth and resulted in a very

good centre for Plymouth, whereas Portsmouth always seemed to be changing their ideas. (*Gladys Sweetnam*)

Commercial Road was widened and slightly straightened after the war, and Palmerston Road rebuilt broader, partly by private enterprise and partly by the council.

They tried to institute some form of regularity of façade, of architectural merit. The [City] Architect of the day would have been the arbiter on those things, and he saw that there was a trend following the use of Portland stone in some of these major porticoes... The east side of Palmerston Road was for the most part 'cost of works payments' that were accredited to property that was already there and rebuilt by virtue of

Handleys, now Debenhams, and the shops on the western side of Palmerston Road built by the council, photographed 1959–60.

C & A's, the first shop to be rebuilt in Commercial Road, shortly before it reopened in 1952. (By courtesy of *The News*)

government grant. The other side was not possible, I think, to get a cohesive redevelopment going on that particular group, on the west side. That is when the city council moved in and bought it. (*Denis Georges, planning dept from 1949*)

Many people were disappointed with the speed and results of the reconstruction.

It was very worrying to see all the bombsites left derelict for so long.... But I remember, for years after the war, I mean, you were still putting in reports as far as police work was concerned, to say, "It was on the bomb site in such-and-such a road"... I've always been upset because of the fact that a lot of properties were demolished that, in this day and age, would never have been demolished because of their

historical interest... I was always disappointed to see places like Hanover Street and Hawke Street. All the houses down there, although a lot of them were damaged very badly, they could have been kept... They had beautiful porticoes; and they had steps that led up to the front door; and they had bow windows and so on. And all that lot was bulldozed down and all these flats were put in their place. (*Ken Hampton, police officer 1930s–'60s*)

Some argue that the concentration on housing worked to the city's advantage in the long run.

... we have actually got umpteen thousand houses rebuilt on the side of Portsdown Hill, we've got about another ten thousand houses we have managed to build at Leigh Park, all of which were

absolutely essential to rehouse the residents of the city who had lost their properties or wanted to come here to work. We've introduced, I think, in the order of a thousand new jobs a year over a 20-odd year period and it is only by doing that we are able to off balance the loss of jobs that came out of the dockyard. From 25,000 down to 2,500 – then you have to make a lot of new jobs available. To do that you have to make sure you have the land, you have to then put the road surfaces and all the superstructures in it. You had your hands full and your finances fully extended to provide housing and jobs. So, yes, a lot of people would have been right to say "your shopping centre was a long time in the making" etc, but when we did come to do it we were able to then look around and see the experiences and the findings of other local authorities and how their new shopping centres were working out. For instance, I wouldn't want a shopping centre like Plymouth anymore. They put a proper gridiron pattern in which didn't lend itself to what I call major pedestrianisation of shopping centres, or provide for the general covered shopping facilities. (*Denis Georges, planning department*)

Portsmouth since the reconstruction

Although some bombsites remained, notably the Guildhall, the reconstruction phase was over by the mid-1950s. The city still had its

Many Victorian houses in central Portsmouth were demolished in the late 1950s and 1960s including these in Mayo Street, photographed in 1969.

problems, however, including large numbers of Victorian houses below contemporary standards. A decision was taken not to rebuild Kings Road as a shopping district.

...we had far too many shopping premises... But the planning policy over the last 40-50 years has been to reduce it, to reduce ribbon shopping development from additional roads. Now Fratton Road is a good example, it used to be shopping all the way from... the major junction in North End all the way down to Fratton Bridge. Well you go down there now and you will see there is quite a large number of residential... There will be further residential infill to combat the lack of need for shopping now the out-of-town shopping centres, the Ocean Parks, Sainsburys at Farlington [exist]. *(Denis Georges, former planning officer, talking in 1995)*

To meet the continuing housing shortage and replace homes lost through comprehensive redevelopment schemes, in the late 1950s and early 1960s the council built a number of high-rise blocks in Portsea and Landport.

Vertical village? Yes, I'm afraid, again, that was following what you might call the trends and the fashion in post-war redevelopments, not only in Portsmouth but throughout the whole of the United Kingdom, where the principle of saving land by building the American style of 'up in the air', saving valuable land space, as opposed to [it] being swallowed by houses, in fact is quite fallacious. You can get very nearly as many properties in properly designed terrace groups as you can in vertical villages. But nevertheless the trend was also supported by government grants in terms of housing subsidy of the day. *(Denis Georges, planning dept from 1949)*

So we took it, and we have been here nearly 33 years... It's lovely at night, because you look out there, and you see all the ships going out, all lit up. It does look nice. We are lucky to be up here.

Mayo Close in 1973, built on the site of Mayo Street, Buckland.

Southsea from the air, 1977. The new tower blocks of Somerstown (top left) contrast with the generously-spaced villas of the 1840s (centre) and gridiron pattern of Victorian terraced houses elsewhere. Palmerston Road is bottom right.

I'd rather be up here than down there anyway. (*Resident of Millgate House, a tower block*)

We lived in Lower Forbury Road... they've pulled that side of Somers Road down to build Winston Churchill Avenue and all the new tower blocks, and we were then moved – we all lived in little terraced houses – to this area. When we came here, this block particularly, even more than the one up in Queen Street, was all the neighbours from our area. Back in 1964, we moved here. It upset a lot of them... As I say, they had lived through the war there. I think they thought the war was the worst thing that was going to happen to them, and suddenly they had to move, and that seemed almost worse... this block [Millgate House] and Sarah Robinson, down in Queen Street, I think may have been the first two tower blocks built in Portsmouth, and they are both built on a girder system. All the other blocks, I think, are built on the same system as the one in London [Ronan Point]... that had a gas explosion and it fell down. When that happened, all the other blocks had to have their gas taken out, and they weren't allowed to have gas any more. We were still allowed to keep gas stoves, if we wanted to, because we were built on this girder system. The one thing you weren't allowed to have, and are still not allowed to have in a tower block is animals, and, of course, we had a cat of 14-years-old. We'd had him since he was a kitten. We'd had his mother before him, and that was very heartbreaking for everybody. You couldn't just desert them. You are not going to find a home for a 14-year-old cat that only likes you anyway. So you have to go and have a healthy animal put to sleep. You didn't meet many of the other people in the block unless they happened to be in the lift. In those days, when we first came here, one lift served the even floors and one lift served the odd floors, and you might never ever meet people who were on the odd floors... everybody who came here were people who had come from ordinary little terraced houses that they had either owned or rented. They weren't actually council tenants. They became council tenants, but

they hadn't been council tenants before. Portsmouth, since the war, has become a gigantic council estate. (*Ruth Williams*)

I moved in with him in his little flat in Southsea, which wasn't big enough for the both of us. We went onto the council list and they offered us two other places, and then they offered us this one and we came to look at it and I was over the moon with it and I said "Oh, yes, I loved it"... To come into the actual flat is what appealed to me... it was certainly massive compared to what we had been living in so we were pleased to move in... all these along this floor are for the mature people. And then there's flats up above that are for the young people with children, which seems odd, you know, that they've just got a little balcony... And a lot of people do complain about the noise of the traffic although it's never worried me... (*Jean Martin-Brennan, resident of Estella Street, flats in Buckland 1990s*)

By 1970 wide-scale demolition and redevelopment was discredited.

And when the areas such as General Improvement Areas were first mooted – we are talking here about the early '60s when it first became the vogue. A lot of people were quick to jump on and said, 'we think this is what should happen now – we don't want to see any more demolition of terraced houses, let's see if we can improve them as they stand"

and that is when new areas were sort of advocated, particular the whole of Stamshaw, parts of Buckland and then large areas south of the railway in terms of Old Fawcett Road and all round there, Somers Road, that part of the area. So in fact we finished up by developing something like 30 General Improvement Areas round the city. (*Denis Georges, planning dept from 1949*)

Another problem was how to modernise the road network, given that access onto Portsea Island was possible only across Portsbridge and the Eastern Road bridge, opened during the war.

So the north-south road was a big debate that took place over 20 years. That was not resolved from 1947 through to 1967, whether we were going to have a major new north-south road. Eventually of course, we decided, yes, we would have one, coming across the mud, through the harbour, in terms of the M275 and that was the wonderful salvation because otherwise it was going to rip the heart out of the whole of Stamshaw. (*Denis Georges, planning dept from 1949*)

... until we had had Market Way constructed, of course, traffic waited in Commercial Road – probably at peak times for up to half an hour. It took an hour to get out of Portsmouth up to the end of the '60s... And so we were looking hard at Stamshaw and then realised there was enormous opportunity for the M275,

Traffic queuing in Northern Parade on its way to Portsbridge, late 1969.

properly sited... So it gave Stamshaw a new life. When you think, the main road into Portsmouth was via Twyford Avenue, which is a gyratory system, and life was impossible for the people who lived there. (*F. Emery-Wallis, Chairman of the Development and Estates committee, 1965–74*)

Renting was the norm for most people before the 1970s. Virtually no private houses were built in Portsmouth from 1945 until about 1966. Then the council changed policy.

...my paternal grandparents had always had the philosophy that owning a house was a "millstone round your neck", which seems incredible in this day and age, but he would be responsible if any repairs were needed, and I think

my father had inherited a certain degree of that... Certainly, initially my father didn't have the financial position to be able to take on that responsibility of a mortgage... (*Jan Ross, child of a council tenant at Leigh Park, 1950s*)

Yes, I moved to Margate Road in Southsea just up from the King's Theatre... They were just bedsits, really, and I was at the top of the house on the third floor. And it was just the bedsit, but you had a, a gas ring for cooking, and you shared bathing facilities... I believe there was a washbasin in my room, so that was very good. And, you know, when you are young it was quite adequate, really. (*Jean Martin-Brennan, occupier of a bedsit, 1953–56*)

The power station was giving over from coal and it no longer needed the land just by the cathedral,

which had these huge dumps of coal, mostly coal dust. We negotiated to buy it, and no one would buy the land, and the housing committee said 'not on your life' we are not going to build houses surrounded by coal. It was an opportunity, and in the end we had to negotiate with the builder and sell him a plot at a time because he thought that no one would buy the [houses]... Then the city bought Victoria Barracks, near Pembroke Park, and I got most of that allocated for private housing. (*F. Emery-Wallis, Chairman of the Development and Estates committee?, 1965–74*)

Another, less successful aspect of Portsmouth's townscape is the Tricorn Centre, opened in 1966.

It was necessary to solve some of the problems in that area north of Charlotte Street. In the first place it was absolutely vital to try to put some sense into what was the wholesale fruit and vegetable market. In my era, even all through the war, I can remember coming down on the bus, down to school... Commercial Road, as far up as Charles Dickens Birthplace, was festooned with early morning traders that had come in from the market gardens in the areas of Titchfield, Fareham, Waterlooville, all with their goods for sale, and the lorries parked up on either side of the road – that was your wholesalers. Your retailers would come along with hundreds of vans and pick what they wanted, sprouts here, cauliflowers there, cabbages, whatever was going, whatever was the mode of that day. We had the whole of this wholesale fruit and veg market taking place on the public highway from the Charles Dickens area of Commercial Road all the way down to Charlotte Street. (*Denis Georges, planning dept from 1949*)

The Tricorn combined car parking, a wholesale fruit and vegetable market on the first floor, a nightclub, some flats and shopping. Unfortunately the shops were never successfully let.

...shopping like the casbah... You go through narrow shopping streets that are very busy and bustling and then you suddenly open out into big squares, and that was the sort of concept of the shopping, and the character of the building... when we started building in 1963 the economy was expanding like anything, it collapsed in 1964. (*Owen Luder, architect of the Tricorn*)

The façade of the Guildhall was rebuilt almost exactly as it had been before the war in 1955-59, and in the early 1970s a new civic area was created around it to the plans of a consultant, Lord Esher. It included the new civic offices.

The old A3 route used to come right down Commercial Road – went past the Guildhall, straight through Portsmouth. There was a great debate on whether or not they wanted to do away with that traffic running through the Guildhall Square. City council had the determination to make that decision and it wasn't an easy one for them to make. There was a lot of local opposition too. Removing, as it were, the view of the Guildhall. (*Denis Georges, planning dept from 1949*)

I do like that very much, because I think the decision to rebuild the Guildhall as it was was a very good one, the decision to surround it with what I think are more interesting

Private housing going up on the site of Victoria Barracks, 1973. The City Museum, converted from a barrack block, is at the foot of the picture.

Paulsgrove House dated back to the 17th century. It was demolished to make way for the M27.

modern buildings, I like all the reflections, I like that dark glass... I like a big empty town square that can be used for various purposes. It's good for ceremonial purposes. (*Pat Haskell*)

Terrible, absolutely terrible, I thought. That was the worst thing they've done to Portsmouth, I think, personally. I mean, when you look back from there we used to see Arundel Street and the station. Now there's only that dreadful civic centre. Appalling! (*Geoff Minter*)

Conclusion

The city is certainly not as it was. Although many now regret the way it has changed, most new developments were accepted at the time as a change for the better, a move forward. It is only in retrospect that the problems that created by new ways of living have been seen as sometimes worse than what had gone before.

Portsea Island from the west, 1983.